DREAM SYMBOLISM

"The House of Sleep" from *De Tempel der Zang-Godinnen,* 1733.

DREAM SYMBOLISM

by

Manly P. Hall

The Philosophical Research Society, Inc.
Los Angeles, California

ISBN NO. 0-89314-392-8
L.C. 79-2420

Fourth Printing
(Formerly published under the title *Studies in Dream Symbolism*)

Library of Congress Cataloging in Publication Data

Hall, Manly Palmer, 1901-
  Dream symbolism.

  Reprint of the ed. published by The Philosophical Research Society, Los Angeles, under
title: Studies in dream symbolism.
  Includes index.
  1. Dreams.   I. Title.

BF1078.H265   1979   154.6'3   79-2420
ISBN 0-89314-392-8

Published by

THE PHILOSOPHICAL RESEARCH SOCIETY, INC.
3910 Los Feliz Boulevard, Los Angeles, CA 90027-2399

Printed in the U.S.A.

TABLE OF CONTENTS

PART I:

THE DREAM PROCESS

From the very dawn of human achievement, dreams have been recorded. Among ancient and primitive societies, one of the duties of the priests, or the spiritual leaders of people, was the interpretation of dreams. It would seem that in these culture groups, the dream was regarded as a genuine psychic phenomenon, and was assumed to have meaning. Meaning, for these people, was a rather literal thing. It had to do with daily occupation and daily problem. The dream also had certain prophetic dimensions, and was held to be a link between the world of the living and the invisible universe that surrounds man.

The Greeks were much inclined toward this point of view. Democritus, whose reputation has been closely associated with his discoveries in the field of atomism, held that the dream represented man's sensitivity, in the sleeping state, to shadows, ghosts, elements and substances floating in the air, perhaps even derived from the consciousness of other persons. He held that space was filled with bodies, many of them fragmentary and gradually disintegrating, and that in sleep man had some participation in this chaotic sphere which was a sort of psychic graveyard.

Aristotle, always a more conservative man, was inclined to suspect that dreams arose within the individual himself due to psychological factors in his own nature, or from environmental pressures affecting the personality. Cicero liked to think that dreams were prophetic, except those after heavy meals, which he doubted could have a divine origin. Plato probably can be summarized as taking the position that dreams were a form of communication between the internal life of man—that is, his soul or psychic content—and his external or physical existence, as impressed upon the brain.

During the medieval period, there was not much additional material contributed to this subject. The Churchmen, who dominated the thinking of the time, were inclined either to follow Aristotle or Plato. During the last three or four hundred years, however, many philosophers have taken an interest in dreams, very often as a means of sustaining other, broader theories with which they were concerned. Gradually their opinions moved toward those now generally held, but we may admit without reservation that even today the dream and the processes by which it is produced are not fully understood.

1

Our word "dream," from medieval English, German, and old Teutonic roots, seems to come from a word which means "to deceive," implying that at a very early time, in European culture certainly, man doubted his dreams, considering them, perhaps, as the productions of some kind of fantasy not entirely within the boundaries of reality. Thus we may say that in the last four thousand years, man has gradually drifted from the belief that a dream was a factual, actual experience occurring in another region or dimension of space, to the concept that the dream was intimately associated with the internal life of the individual. This is a broad statement, and is subject to some modifications, but for our purposes, it will indicate the general direction of thinking.

Dreaming in man is associated with age patterns. We know that children do dream, and that their dreams are rather easy to interpret because they generally arise from a comparatively small area of stimulation. There are only certain things meaningful or comprehensible to the child, and it has only an elementary group of symbols with which to react to stimulation. In the case of the aged, dreams lose most of their vitality in the majority of instances. They are not as numerous, nor as intense, nor as well remembered. Therefore, we may assume that certain psychological processes associated with age have a tendency to diminish dream intensity.

The majority of important dreaming takes place during the period between adolescence and the older years, or what might be termed the mature years. There is a grave question, however, whether maturity in the sense of time has very much to do with it. More likely, it is maturity in the sense of activity. The adult person is living a more strenuous life, particularly in a competitive society. He is under more psychic tension; more subject to the alternations of success and failure, of hope and despair. He is more afflicted by worry and fear, and in the modern world, he is considerably agitated by world conditions beyond his power to influence or modify. The fact that dreaming is most frequent in the years of maturity and maximum activity may well imply that the dream arises as the personality becomes more complex and more laden with the productions of its own actions and reactions.

We can extend this thought a little further by considering the life of domestic animals. We know that animals dream, and it has been observed that this dreaming becomes more noticeable as the animal ascends the scale of intelligence. We also note that dreams are more frequent in animals with active lives than those with sedentary lives. The family lap dog is not a prolific dreamer, and his dreams, if he has any, appear to be comparatively moderate. Occasionally he will flick a leg in his sleep or appear to be munching a particularly fine bone, but other than that, we do not see too much dream symbolism. The hunting dog, however, will nearly always show strong signs of dream excitement after a hunt. Dogs that are engaged in various services for man—as for instance, police dogs or seeing-eye dogs that have to fight with traffic to protect their masters, and apparently develop a very keen sense of canine responsibility—such dogs dream more frequently. Thus responsibility, or the sense of urgency or of hazard, as experienced consciously, seem to affect the unconscious state of the animal.

Another point that might be made in passing concerns dreams in those who are in one way or another curiously afflicted. It is not as yet demonstrated that persons born blind have visual dreams. The tendency is definitely to suggest that they do not; that where they do have dream experiences, these take other forms, making use of symbolism in areas where sensory perceptions are still available. This is not true, however, if the individual becomes blind after once having become aware of the world around him. Persons who are born deaf are not known to have dreams involving speaking of words or other phenomena with which they are not familiar. It is reported that after Helen Keller had been taught to speak, speech began to occur in her dreams. Prior to her own experience of speech, however, this did not occur. Points of this kind continually indicate some valid relationship between phenomena as experienced by the senses and the mysteries of sleep phenomena as recorded in dreams.

Dream phenomena are now generally regarded as of two kind: those arising in the environment around man, by means of which his rest is in some way partly disturbed, and those of an essentially internal origin, arising distinctly within the individual and having no obviously valid relationship to immediate circumstances of his external life. Undoubtedly, however, many of the dreams of internal origin are ultimately related to environmental circumstances.

The first of these groups would arise from the individual taking his daily activities into rest with him. Therefore, the dream in most cases can be directly traced, if not to the circumstances of the preceding day, at least to a series of pressing circumstances that have occurred recently, or which represent the natural probable human reaction to fear, worry, tension, or anxiety of some kind. This group would also include such dreams as may arise from digestive difficulties, when the origin is definitely physical, perhaps in the form of mince pie or broiled lobster late at night. I think we can include with environmental dreams all dream phenomena that arise from environment, whether immediate or remote; whether it be something brought forward from childhood, or something that has occurred within the last few hours before sleep. All of these, generally, belong to one classification, broken up into time groupings.

The internal type of dream would appear to be considerably detached from such considerations, having no essential relationship to any immediate, or even remote, known event. It may be regarded as indication of the pressures of basic temperament. What the individual is begins to press itself upon his awareness, and he is explaining or interpreting himself. Therefore, the internal group can be said to be composed of what the individual is, and the result of what he does.

These two general classifications are now believed to explain most dream phenomena. We can, however, add to these classifications in several ways. We still have a whole group of dreams of a prophetic or mystical nature, which are not fully understood. The materialistic psychologist wishes to classify them with the general body of dreams, assuming that they are only a specialized type of reaction to the pressures of circumstances. The mystic, however, is inclined to feel that the mystical dream, or the mystical experience in itself, is valid; that it represents a direct contact with some superior level of intelligence or consciousness, but that this contact takes upon itself the familiar dream symbols in the process of moving into objective awareness. Therefore, the symbolism may not be essentially different, but the level and quality of the meaning behind the symbols can be very different. Research in this field, as might be expected, is not abundant, but there is an increasing tendency to become concerned about it.

A new factor has also been imposed in recent years under the general heading of environmental dreams as a result of studies in atomism and the development of electronics and related sciences. It is now recognized that there is the possibility of universal pressure upon the individual. Universal processes, chemical, electrical or magnetic, may affect the individual and cause a kind of dreaming that is not related either to the ordinary environment or to the individual's own psychic content. This may open a comparatively large field of research, and is beginning to take considerable significance in our thinking.

Experience has taught men from the very beginning that certain kinds of dreams were dreams of communication. Many of the world's choicest secrets have been discovered as the result of dreams; and some disasters have been averted by dreams. A vast amount of knowledge that we now consciously hold came to us first as the result of sleep phenomena. I think if we removed from the history of knowledge all forms of scientific, philosophic, religious, cultural, artistic, esthetic, or even trade skills, that had first been revealed by dreams, we would still be in a rather primitive condition. The ancients held that most knowledge came from the gods; that man was first instructed by divine beings; and this is little more than saying that this knowledge came to man not merely from his own experience, but by revelation. The dream is therefore a valid form of revelation, and has always been so regarded.

Another phase of the dream problem that perhaps will have to be ultimately explored is the relationship between the dream per se and what we call *daydreaming*. We are constantly playing with symbols, whether we are asleep or awake. When we misunderstand our neighbor, for example, and blame him for something that was not his meaning, we are actually involved in the same process as dream interpretation. We are dreaming awake, because we are calling forth these symbolic shadows and attempting to use them in the grasping of ideas.

Daydreaming, of course, has as its fundamental principle a kind of escape mechanism. The daydreamer is a person trying to live in a private world. Not getting along too well in the public regions in which he abides, he decides that it would be more pleasant and more comfortable for him to invent a world. And he invents as diligently as any author of fiction or fantasy. He invents a world in which he is always right. Now, this is a delightful state of affairs; the only difficulty with it is that it is a delusion and a snare because it assumes something that cannot be assumed—namely, that he is always right. This need to be always right is associated with certain weaknesses of his temperament; whatever the psychological handicaps of his life may be, they are always neutralized in the daydream. The individual finds himself, therefore, always an object of admiration. He is not only always right, but he is always magnificent. He is also privileged to exercise authorities and freedoms that are not possible in his daily life.

So in daydreaming, we develop all kinds of utopias, based upon almost any subject, from retiring into a monastery in the Himalayas to becoming a beachcomber in Tahiti. Whatever seems to bring us freedom from the pressures that affect us, and for which we are not able to make adequate compensatory adjustments—whatever gives us a sense of total sufficiency, is in some way shadowed in our daydreams. The daydream can therefore be analyzed to the end of determining the inadequacies or imperfections of our own psychic processes. In the daydream, we consciously build; in the ordinary dream, we unconsciously build; but in both cases, we are working with the same basic materials. And that which we build will also tell a story of ourselves. We know the architect by his house. We know the individual's nature by what he seeks to achieve and what he seeks to escape. These may be clearly indicated in his daydreaming or in his dreaming.

It would seem that the psychological sleep consciousness of man is more active now than ever before in our recorded history, implying that the average person is more psychically stress-ridden than ever before. The insecurities of life are accumulating more rapidly than they used to, and where this situation is not met with some appropriate remedy, nervous breakdowns are almost certain, heart trouble is more frequent, and in spite of our elaborate scientific discoveries and the ways in which we can now combat many ailments, the public health is not as good as it was fifty years ago. Length of life in some cases is greater, but it may be merely an extended period of time for acute mental anguish.

Bearing these factors in mind, we can see why many persons should have disturbed rest. This disturbance is of several kinds. Some people cannot seem to sleep at all; others sleep only fitfully. Some have the sense of dreaming, but do not remember the dream. Of the dreams that are remembered, more and more are ominous and unpleasant; they do not have much of contentment in them. They are not the dreams of the happy child to be found in some fairy tale. They are the dreams that come close to nightmares—dreams in which man continues to experience the difficulties, perhaps intensified, by which his daily life is so unhappily punctuated.

When dreaming is a more or less symbolic continuation of the lines of thought with which the individual was previously concerned, it is an indication that he is under continuous tension. A general interpretation of such dreams, from the standpoint of self-help, is simply that the person is not able to disentangle himself sufficiently from his own physical and mental preoccupations to relax even when he is asleep.

Thus an individual's sleep pattern is closely related to his psychological integration. If a person awakens reasonably refreshed from sleep, when his dreams are few, or when at least he has no memory of them, it is a fair indication that his pressures are not too great. We wonder sometimes if a certain type of sleep fatigue does not really testify to unremembered sleep activity. In other words, we may not have any remembrance of a dream, but if we wake up in the morning feeling that sleep has not refreshed us, and we get out of bed as tired as when we went to bed, and there are no physical symptoms of illness to support the feeling, then it is quite possible that this lassitude is due to an intense sleep phenomenon that is not remembered. So if you wake up in the morning with the feeling that you have just finished a nine-round fight, without having any memory of the fight but with the full measure of exhaustion and a certain degree of psychic scarring, it is quite possible that there has been very little rest due to psychic pressure.

It seems to me that one of the proofs that the individual's pressures are not too great for him is that he can lie awake without sleeping, but resting and in bed, for eight hours, without a negative thought. If when he rests, his natural thoughts are pleasant, gentle, non-destructive; or if he can carry lightly through the hours some pleasant project that he hopes to advance; if he can maintain a subtle positivity without straining the mind, and advance the solution of his own problems without pressure or tension—if he can do this, the chances are that his nervous system is under control.

We know that sleep implies a certain therapy; that it is quite possible that in sleep, through dreams, things confused or obscured become clarified. We also know that the subconscious or subjective part of man is more available to influence during sleep than in his waking state. Thus, the door that leads into the world of sleep, leads into many mysteries, into strange paths and byways, about which we know comparatively little.

PART II:

THE SLEEP PHENOMENON

Sleep phenomena have always been associated with oracles. We find evidence of this among practically all primitive peoples, and records have descended from the more advanced culture groups. Sleep was regarded as a magic condition. It was in some way a suspension of the outer life. It was assumed that the soul could depart from the body, visit remote regions, and ascend through the various orbits of the world to come close to the divine principles at the root of life. Because dream phenomena were so obviously not of this world, it was assumed that there was another world in which dreams were real. In the ancient Greek art, there were representations of the gate of sleep, which led from the mortal estate into a strange temple where shadowy phantom forms lurked in the gloom, or performed weird, ritualistic dances around the altars of some ancient deity.

It was not, however, in Greek culture alone that sleep gained the strong oracular authority that later came to be associated with it. Sleep was not only natural, but could be induced by artificial means. Very far back, men developed the hypnotic arts, although they did not know them by such a name. They found ways to induce artificial sleep, and to throw a subject into a state of somnambulism. At Delphi, the greatest of all the Grecian oracles, a kind of trance or ecstasy was induced by vapors rising from a deep vent in the earth. These vapors had an intoxicating effect, and when the priestess was seated on her tripod over this vent, she inhaled the fumes and passed into a strange half-sleeping condition. While in this state, she would give forth the oracles, or the messages from the deities, in the form of hexameter verse. In the ancient grotto of Trophonius, another celebrated oracle of the time, those seeking answers to their questions were conducted down into a cave-like place. Here they were either exposed to some natural fume that intoxicated the mind, or possibly were given drugs to induce visions.

Drugs for this purpose are well known, perhaps the most spectacular example being the use of hashish by the sect of the Assassins in Iraq. Here a very powerful drug brought with it extraordinary ocular hallucination, causing those who took it to believe that they had been transported into the paradise promised by Mohammed in the Koran. Drugs were used by the Druids, and various incenses are frequently referred to.

8

And in one early work, it is mentioned that some of the heretical Christian sects of the first few centuries were accused of drugging the communion cup in order to produce ecstasies and trances, during which religious experiences were recorded. The American Indian induced a form of hypnotic trance by moving an eagle feather back and forth before the eyes of the subject. These trances could also be induced by music, or by various forms of ritualism, some of which have descended to us in the excitements and ecstasies of the Holy Rollers and other groups of Adventists.

In addition to these means, sleep phenomena could be effected by the use of certain foods or exercises or disciplines, producing a curious kind of fatigue, or by fasting, which resulted in a general weakening of the body. The principle behind fasting has been known since the dawn of time, and was practiced by nearly all primitive peoples long before they had any theology or philosophy such as we know. The experience of fasting led to one inevitable conclusion—namely, that as the power of the body energies was depleted, the individual became more sensitive to superphysical experiences. By fasting, he had cleansed the body of the toxins that are one of the causes of psychic tension and irritation. The theory was that the reduction of the body awareness with which we are so much concerned, is accompanied by the reduction of the body complaint that is constantly and insidiously encroaching upon our consciousness, and the lowering of the bodily vitalities that impel us to various excesses of action. All this left the person weak and drowsy, uncertain of his own objectivity. It was easier for him to sleep in this state, and he found that his sleeping had a certain clarity which was not common where the body was laden with physical impurities.

Thus we see that from an early time, men sought to induce artificial sleep, or in one way or another to destroy the normal equilibrium of man's objective awareness, because in this state he was held to have a peculiar proximity to spiritual mysteries. The motive was quite sincere. These people believed that it was the only way to open the door to that other world of spiritual essences which was closed to man by the ordinary orientation of his sensory perceptions.

It was early assumed that the dream world was similar to the world of the dead. Man asleep appeared to be dead, but was not really so. Death was a long sleep; sleep was a little death. St. Paul points this out when he says, ''I die daily.'' This concept of the mystery of sleep, with its power to break through, seems to have affected our psychology and our general attitude toward life, and to have descended subtly to us in a number of our beliefs, superstitions, and legends.

We can divide our thinking on this subject into two very broad patterns. The first, and one that is still held by many mystics, is that essentially the old concept was correct—that sleep does mysteriously liberate the soul from the body, if not totally, at least sufficiently to give the soul a more positive existence while the body is at rest. East Indian metaphysics also intimates this concept that the soul can temporarily leave the body and can have adventures and experiences that may later be brought through into remembrance, or partly so, although some elements may elude us as we return to the waking state.

The other school of thought affirms that the phenomenon of the dream can be rationally explained on a psychological level. According to this view, the soul does not actually leave the body, but the psychic nature comes into a new relationship with the personality during sleep. In sleep, the objective person is in a state of almost complete suspension of animation, and the outer world loses its power to impress and influence us. We appear to be temporarily free from the burden of even our own opinions. A quietude descends upon the mind and emotions, and this quietude makes possible man's sensing of deeper phases of his own life. It permits certain currents to seemingly reverse themselves, so that instead of man receiving his principal stimulation from the outside, he suddenly becomes passive and experiences life moving from within himself. An inner world imposes itself upon the outer world; whereas in the waking state, this imposition from within is made comparatively impossible by the activity of the objective faculties.

Even in sleep, man has certain kinds of awareness, but these are more subtle than the awareness of the waking state. Parapsychology researches suggest the possibility that in the sleep state, man may attain a certain clairvoyance, a certain increased clairsentience, a telepathic rapport with other persons. In sleep, he may sense more acutely the thoughts of his neighbors, friends, and associates. He may be more responsive intuitively to the temperaments of those around him. He may also receive into himself masses of telepathic fragments from the lives and thoughts and emotions of countless persons. These may or may not have any general meaning, but under some conditions, they may also assume prophetic proportions.

In this same general area, it is quite conceivable that man can attune himself to some kind of a record that remains in space around him at all times. We are not sure that space is non-intellectual. We are not sure that the air around us is not mental atmosphere. We cannot be certain that nature itself does not have its own thinking, and that in a receptive mood, we may tune in to these larger thoughts—thoughts which perhaps we can later interpret in genius and great artistry. There seems to be a tendency, also, for this receptivity to become conditioned by certain major phases of our interests. We know that if we take certain thoughts to sleep, we may have dream experiences relating to these thoughts. We also recognize the age-old custom of taking problems to sleep, with the idea that in the morning we will awaken with the answer; and many have had this experience. Great artists, musicians, and scientists have generally admitted the importance of sleep phenomena in the advancements of their various abilities. Musicians have heard their melodies in sleep or dreams, or trance-like states. Artists have seen the pictures which they would later place upon canvas.

Sleep seems to approximate the state of consciousness attained through the disciplines of meditation and the various retrospective and contemplative exercises of the Greek theory and of the East Indian schools. These meditations are quietudes, leading finally to an almost complete submersion of the personal consciousness in a deep and mysterious ocean of universal value, such as is intimated in the samadhi of Vedanta, or the mysterious nirvanic trances of the Buddhist arhats.

Let us think through for a moment the Chinese, Greek and Egyptian belief that in sleep, the soul of man passes into the after-death state; that sleeping is in reality a kind of focusing of man's consciousness on another plane of function. During this sleep experience, the psychic nature may have certain temporary experiences that parallel the after-death state. The Egyptians, who were very thoughtful about this, have given us quite an exhaustive concept of the afterlife. They implied, for example, that in the afterlife, the individual was punished or rewarded according to certain merits or demerits. Punishment consisted of a process of cleansing similar to the concept of the Christian purgatory, which merely means purging of the life of its various negative attributes. In the underworld of the Egyptians, the soul is constantly being tried or tested in the great court of the gods—the principal episode being the psychostasia, or the weighing of the soul. The Egyptians tell us, therefore, that death is a process by which consciousness is brought into the presence of punishment and reward. To a smaller degree, then, may not the sleep phenomenon carry somewhat of this burden?

Psychologists tell us that during sleep, in dreams, the individual certainly comes face to face with phases or aspects of his own submerged personality. And the psychological dream is usually one of a basically corrective nature. It is a punishment experience, an experience in which the individual faces some part of himself that he rejects, or that is hidden from his awareness, during his daily conscious life. Most psychological dreams tell us that there is something wrong with the person; and as we know that the average person does not live an entirely proper life, that he is not always right, and that his conduct is not always above reproach, we can quite readily understand that his mistakes, his false beliefs and unreasonable opinions that influence his conduct—all these can and usually do produce a psychological backlog that becomes locked in him, and this is available to him most directly either through sleep or through what is called reverie, a process resembling sleep, where the individual becomes relaxed or receptive to the impressions of his own psychic life.

The essential concepts of the Egyptians might not be so different, therefore, from many of the opinions we hold today. But because the Egyptians put their thoughts into a highly theological language, we are inclined to regard their feelings as merely a survival of primitive religious doctrine. Actually, the fundamental point involved is that sleep and death, being aspects of one general condition, are phases of human existence in which punishment and reward play a distinct part.

Thus the idea that the sleep life is a place of purging has some very definite validity. We know that we can be punished by our own memories. The things we have done are never totally forgotten. The mistakes we make, injuries that we cause, all leave markings in our remembrance, and these, in turn, may arise or be re-activated to give us pangs of conscience or guilt mechanisms of one kind or another. If we blocked the memory of man, a large part of psychotherapy would be unnecessary. It is memory that actually undoes us, forcing us to face our past conduct and to compare this conduct with its own consequences and the misfortunes that have ensued.

We know that dreaming existed long before men had any conscious knowledge of psychotherapy. The dream preceded any formularized concept by means of which psychotherapy could have been influenced into existence. The individual was not originally taught that his dreaming was important; he had the dreams, and he felt their importance; and gradually, from this feeling, he has developed his reaction to sleep phenomena in general.

It is possible, then, that sleep is a way of bringing the individual into more immediate realization of his own character. Perhaps in sleep the individual must come nearer to living with himself than at any other time; he comes in contact with a kind of self which he might otherwise never know to exist. In our daily objective lives, we are living largely by patterns and pressures, and we are conscious because of the continual excitation of the central nervous system. If we always lived objectively, in a waking state, it is quite probable that many of our faults would never be corrected. It may well be, therefore, that sleep is important to us not only as a means of physical relaxation, but as a means of continuing the processes of psychological adjustment by which our characters are brought into harmony with our ethical convictions.

The psychological procedures used today are indicating that this theory is essentially true. For one reason or another, the psychologist has hit upon the dream as one of his most valuable instruments, and he frequently uses methods that tend to stimulate the dream processes, causing the patient to have significant dreams. This is why a person who has not usually dreamed much will begin to dream more frequently and more intensely under analysis. Having been stirred by analysis or investigation, the subconscious suddenly becomes increasingly active, apparently aware that it will now be regarded.

We also think of the dream experience as one means of exhausting certain types of pressures. This process of cleaning out the subconscious by bringing its content into objectivity is to a measure a way of attaining virtue. Outwardly, we are not necessarily logical or consistent in action; nor are we sufficiently observant to consciously record the various happenings that mark the day. In sleep, however, it is as though a judge sat upon a bench, weighing and estimating the processes by which our mental and emotional actions have been stimulated. Our motives are more carefully analyzed. The various secret desires or feelings that we have carefully hidden from other people are suddenly exposed to us.

Dreaming appears to arise especially in connection with a certain neurotic type of attitude. The individual who senses guilt, who blames himself, or who feels that some mysterious force operating through his own personality is injuring him—this kind of person most frequently dreams. Also, this person finds dreams more important to him. Many individuals do dream, but pay no particular attention to the dreams. They assume that an occasional dream is natural; therefore they think very little about it. If, however, the person is introverted or inhibited, the very processes that make him think too much about himself, also cause him to think too much about his dreams. Thus, the dreams become increasingly important as he tries to understand them, and he nearly always tries to understand them in a negative way, as though they implied guilt or testified to some false attitude or error of conduct on his own part.

The dream experience is therefore a key to the waking experience, revealing, in a mysterious way, the secrets of our daily life. By his sleep, man solves the mystery of his waking hours, and discovers the importance of events that might otherwise pass unnoticed. Thus, to the Greeks, sleep was part of an acceptance into the temple or sanctuary of realities. It was quite conceivable to them, and to many others, that sleep phenomena could be more valid than waking phenomena.

The modern person would probably consider this to be a little better than an absurdity. But is it absurd? Does the psychologist, when he explores the dream symbolism of a patient, discover that the patient possesses a knowledge greater than what he consciously knows he possesses? Is the dream more honest than our daily conduct? Does it reveal truths of which we are not consciously aware? If such is the case, then the dream is instructive, and does represent a valid source of knowledge. It can be a means of discovering values that might otherwise never be recognized, because in the complexity of our waking consciousness, our sense of values is frequently distorted or in one way or another confused.

The psychologist may agree that all this is evidently true, but he may hold the position that it is possible simply because the subconscious part of man is essentially wiser than the conscious; that the subconscious has a skill that could be very obvious. Most of the things we do in life, we do for the advantage of our temporal, objective state. The individual is selfish, unkind, cruel, gossipy, worrisome, angry, because these conditions are part of his objective, waking way of life. They seem to be justified by the things that happen to him. They seem to be made necessary by the kind of world in which he lives. The question then arises—does this inner or subconscious part of man, this subjective self, have the same requirements, the same attitudes, and the same convictions? For instance, can the subjective part of man be bound to a creed, even though his objective mind may be so bound? Will the objective part of man be able to free itself from the dogmatism of opinion as easily as this unconscious internal part?

The answer appears to be that while the objective man is a conformist, the psychic being within him remains forever curiously individualistic. This psychic part of man's nature does not become as conditioned by externals as does his objective consciousness. This may be due to a different distribution of sensory perceptions, for it is true that man's eyes, because of their peculiar relationship to phenomena, have given him a strong sense of material reality; whereas the psychic life, observing things not by the eyes, but by some intuitive or internal measure of knowing, may not be so easily over-influenced, confused, or distorted in its judgment.

Unless there were some part in man better than the parts we generally know, there could be no reason for true conscience. If the individual did not have a conflict arising between his actions and the principles that he inwardly holds to be true, he would probably have very few psychic disturbances. It is because somewhere in him there is a better self that he can come into conflict with this better self. He also derives from it the impetus to self-improvement. There has to be something that is stronger than what we are, or we would remain what we are. There has to be some factor in our life that is dissatisfied with our present conduct, or we will never improve. Therefore, within this dissatisfied inner something, there must be a vision of betterness, a sense of betterness, even a knowing of betterness, superior to that with which we face daily life.

The ancients, perhaps from this circumstance alone, contemplated the superiority of the soul over the body. Consequently, we can see why the Hindus, the Greeks, the Egyptians, the Persians, and most other peoples have sensed that the journey of man inward to communion with his own soul was essentially a journey in the direction of betterment. For the soul within man was nearer to the Divine than the objective faculties. Perhaps the Greeks would have said that being nearer to the Divine really meant being closer to the understanding of the laws governing matter and mind and substance and essence. Thus they believed that the soul had a superior power to cognize value, and because of this, it was the natural shepherd or priest of the body.

If all these speculations are old, they are also surprisingly new, because of this point that we have attempted to make—namely, that almost all psychotherapy takes it for granted that the disturbance of man's outer nature arises from disturbances of his psychic life. Disturbance is conflict, and if the psychic life were identical with the objective life, there would be no reason for conflict. In a family, if a parent, having a greater wisdom, beholds in a child an action contrary to its good, it becomes his duty to in some way instruct or correct that child. In the same way, it is forever the duty of the psychic self to instruct or correct the body, the personality, and the objective mind. And where the body and the mind depart from ways of righteousness, the soul communicates its displeasure by a series of intensive symbolic experiences, most often manifested in dreams. Thus, perhaps the modern and the old meet. We are dealing with different words, but with essentially the same ideas.

We have already mentioned the fact that the psychic life apparently is better able to reach man during sleep than at any other time, because during this period, the objective dissenter is temporarily suspended. As Buddha points out, the machinery of the sensory perceptions having ceased, man is relieved of the pressure of the appearances of things. He is relieved of the feeling, which most people have, that what he sees is true. The individual who says, "These things I have seen; these things which I do not like, or which may not be good, are nevertheless true because I have recorded them; and I have recorded them exactly and precisely with the assistance of the sensory perceptions;" — this person is in a highly defensive position. He finds it necessary to live in conformity with these testimonies of things seen and heard and known through immediate contact. Yet these things in themselves are highly relative. Even one careful thought about the world we live in will reveal to us that the conduct of creatures of our own kind is more unreasonable, more inconsistent, and more fantastic than a nightmare. Actually, many of these things that we see and accept as realities because they are occurring in our physical experience, are completely unreasonable; and as far as validity is concerned, they are not by any means actually true. Yet we have a kind of truth based upon external, material experience.

This kind of truth can be important, but only if we light it from within ourselves. Yet we are not all able to take things that happen to us and make them be the immedite cause of conscious growth. Nature is concerned with the advancement of the consciousness of beings; yet man can live for many years, sometimes an entire lifetime, without ever having truly accepted the challenge of the experiences that have occurred to him. He passes through these things—he either enjoys them or he suffers from them, and he goes no further in his estimation. He is definitely opposed to that which hurts him; he is definitely desirous of cultivating that which pleases him. And beyond these attitudes, there is very little logic.

Actually, therefore, man's hope of gaining the necessary experience from action is that this experience be justly measured, weighed, and estimated by some faculty in himself. Plato regarded this faculty as the soul. He believed that the soul is the power by which essential meaning is contributed to experience. Now, essential meaning is very different from apparent meaning, for we can create, and have created, two kinds of codes. One is the code of man, and the other is the code of God or nature. One may be regarded as the code of sacred things, and the other, of profane things. For the most part, man has not built the material way of life upon a divine code. He has built it very largely upon a pattern of compromises down through time—compromises that are never entirely satisfactory and are frequently the cause of his troubles. Yet there may be another code known to himself—whether he realizes that he knows it or not—and this is the code of inevitables as they exist in a larger pattern of life. There is a pattern of law that must be fulfilled. We may break all kinds of man-made rules and survive, but if we break this rule that is not made by man, but has an eternity in existence itself, then we come under serious difficulties. Nature will never rest until we have remedied this break and have returned to a proper and harmonious relationship with the essential pattern of life.

The dream phenomenon seems to have a bearing on this. It seems to be a way of bringing man back to the responsibilities of his life. We know that the sleep process is accompanied by a diminution of the entire excitation processes of the brain and central nervous system. In sleep, we react less violently to stimuli of all kinds. There is a noticeable tendency for the heart to beat less rapidly. There is a very definite shift in the processes of metabolism, which slow down distinctly. We also recognize that there is a gradual separation of energy from the motor system, with the tendency of the body to become inert. And, most of all, of course, we notice that this process gradually ends in the suspension of our objective mental function.

The study of sleep in animals and lower creatures brings some interesting information to our attention. The kind of sleep that we have seems to be peculiar to higher forms of animal life. It is true that all creatures probably rest in some way, but as we go down the ladder of living creatures, we find more of rest and less of sleep. We find that the sleep process is not accompanied by the total extinction of consciousness that we find in man and the higher animals. Thus it might conceivably be that lower forms of life do not require sleep, and that sleep as we know it, is in some way a psychic necessity; that it is necessary only to creatures in whose experience there is a conflict between their way and the universal way.

Animals—and the lower kingdoms of nature particularly—live in such a consistent adjustment with instinct that it is very rare indeed for them to violate it. Man is continually violating it, or has so reconditioned instinct that he cannot depend upon it. Thus, where the creature does not come into any ordinary conflict with nature, apparently there is far less wear and tear on the nervous system, and therefore far less need for sleep as we know it. Animals rest a great deal, but they have the wonderful habit of resting with one eye open. A cat will be very quiet, and you will think that it has been asleep for hours, but if there is the slightest indication of the unusual, a cat's eyes open immediately. It does not shake itself and wake up—it just simply has never lost consciousness of its environment. The same is true of many other animals. Some animals sleep standing up, indicating that they do not need the total relaxation of the motor system. An animal can rest, and it appears to relax completely, but it does not pass into this peculiar coma-like state with which we associate human sleep.

Some of the higher mammals do sleep, but they are also the ones that are now being noted to possess neurotic tendencies; and as a result of association with man for some time, a number of animals have become violently ill. There is now evidence that we may need to develop animal psychologists—not because the animal is of its own nature psychotic, but because experiments have shown that if you subject an animal—as for example, a rat—to incredible wear and tear in the form of confusion, it will become neurotic and begin to show all kinds of symptoms by which it becomes more intimately associated with the human type.

Psychological studies and experiments point to certain conclusions about the relationship between environment and neurosis. It seems evident, for example, that continuous noise, the unexpected breaking of rhythms, inconsistent situations, and the constant violation of law and order in the normal activities of living—these types of stress definitely contribute to the development of neuroses in animals. This could apply to our way of life also, and might help to explain why we become neurotic. A neurosis is usually accompanied by some interesting side effects. Neurotic creatures get tired—not physically tired particularly, but nervously exhausted; they need much more sleep. Also, their appetites change; they usually eat more. They may also become more and more dependent upon various forms of stimulation in order to keep the organism functioning.

With the neurotic individual, sleep apparently becomes nature's method of compensating for tension. This may well explain why the human being and other higher animals require sleep. It is a way of compensating for emergency, for stress, for any form of unusual activity suddenly thrust upon the person. If an animal is placed in a new environment, it will adjust; if this environment is changed with reasonable regularity, it will continue to adjust; but if the changes are unreasonably rapid, the animal becomes neurotic. This, again, may be applied to our way of life, in which our concept of progress makes it necessary to adjust to constantly changing values and securities. As certain types of stress become increasingly frequent or powerful, it is natural that the sleep process should become increasingly necessary and important.

The sleeping and waking cycle with man is obviously associated with the rhythm of the world around him. It has now been rather generally acknowledged that the sleep phenomenon is one of the legitimate links between man and universal phenomena. Even the most skeptical thinker today is inclined to believe that sleeping and waking are tied closely to the light and darkness phenomena of the solar system. Night is a very important factor, not only because of darkness and the limitations imposed upon the activities of man but because it represents the loss of a kind of energy that is present during the daytime as one of the elements of sunlight. The loss of sunlight is not only a symbol, but a factual loss in the vitality of the individual, for his vital resources increase in daylight and decrease in darkness. This is factual, because light contains a stimulating factor. When this is obscured by darkness, there seems to be a distinct change in the energy vibration upon which the individual depends for his survival.

This process has a great deal of meaning, so let us explore it a little further. If you take away the objective consciousness of man, you then reveal something in man that is otherwise concealed. This objective consciousness is so positive, so aggressive, and so active that we are not aware of the passive processes in man. They are always operating, but we do not know it. Now, take away light from an area of the earth, and you remove what might be equivalent to the objective energy of man. The moment this happens, another kind of energy takes over—an energy that has always been present, but has been obscured because the solar energy is far more positive. In the absence of the solar energy, this other energy is more immediately noticeable, and of course, it is not counteracted as it is in the daytime. At night, in other words, the energy of darkness is not overcome by the energy of light; the sword of the sunray no longer slays the dragon of darkness.

Now, if you take away the solar light, what other energy to you release? Of course, the most common thought would be lunar energy, because we know that the lunar energy is real, and that it affects, among other things, the tides. But we also know that the lunar energy is inconsistent, because the moon passes through phases, so we must look for something even more basic to explain the night energy. And we come to one almost certain and inevitable conclusion—namely, that the earth itself has an energy; that there is a kind of vitality that moves outward from the surface of the earth.

We know that the earth is a mysterious electro-chemical structure, and that it does emanate a kind of energy. That this energy emanating from the earth was known to antiquity, we are certain; and it is also recorded for us that this is a somatic energy, an energy that causes drowsiness and carries within it a high content of psychic toxin. The earth energy, therefore, probably has very little to contribute to the true psychic life of man. We know that the earth energy helps to build up bodily structure, and that the solar energy is more stimulating, more irritating, and more involved in the processes of the central nervous system. Experiments in treating tuberculosis by sunlight are a point in this. In other words, the solar energy is an activating energy; the lunar energy is a periodic or cyclic energy; and the earth's energy is almost purely physical, and therefore has its direct effect upon the physical organism. It is therefore quite possible that during the sleep process, part of the remedial agency accompanying rest is due to the fact that the earth energy, liberated from the domination of the solar intensity, does help to restore the material parts of the human constitution. This energy helps to nourish and feed the physical factors that are essential to survival, but it has very little part to play in the psycho-mental life of the human being.

Thus the earth energy is related largely to growth, and the solar energy is related largely to function. Growth has to do with the restoration of the exhausted processes and materials of the body, whereas function has to do with continually exhausting these resources. Man is therefore established in a certain equilibrium between these two. The animal, having practically no intellectual life as we know it, does not exhaust psychic energy the way man does. Therefore, while it lives in both light and darkness, as does the human being, it is able to achieve a more consistent rest; and because it is far more physically polarized than man, it may also have greater nocturnal activity, which we recognize in a number of animals.

It has been assumed that sleep is merely a periodic need of the body, and that it is due almost entirely to the individual exhaustion of resources. But by studying the matter carefully, we realize that the night worker, who must sleep in the daytime, is not in as good a psychological condition as the day worker. Now, this does not mean that all night workers will become neurotic, but it does mean that they are working contrary to this peculiar atmospheric chemistry of day and night. We have already mentioned that during the night hours, the metabolic processes of the individual are lowered. Whereas it may require 200 to 250 calories to animate him for an hour in the waking state, it may require only 100 or 150 calories to accomplish this in the sleeping state. But this same lowering of metabolic process is noted in the case of night workers. We might think that their metabolic processes should be lower in sleep during the daytime, but this does not happen. The metabolism goes down at night for either the day worker or the night worker, indicating that this process lies outside of the body of the individual, and is related to some other procedures operating in nature. Thus, sleep probably has a number of factors involved in its causation.

Now, the sleep phenomenon has a number of different divisions within itself. We have always thought of the individual as being either awake or asleep. While this may be true in a general way, we are sometime going to discover that the term *sleep* covers a wide variety of different processes, not all of which operate in exactly the same way in different persons. There are levels of sleep; the house of sleep has many rooms—not merely this one departure from objectivity. We can note a number of constitutional peculiarities in sleep, and the old star-gazers came to some conclusions about these, which are worth mentioning. One theory is that the sleep processes of individuals are influenced by the positions of planets in their nativities, and that persons with certain positions of planets have difficulty sleeping in various parts of the night and have essentially different sleep rhythms.

We like to believe, for example, that everyone should have about eight hours of sleep; that they should go to bed around ten o'clock, and get up around six-thirty or seven, and that this constitutes the good old-fashioned agrarian pattern based on the importance of milking the cow at the right time. Actually, this is one of the imaginary rules that man has created. A number of persons, particularly of certain temperaments, find that eight hours of sleep will not suffice them; others find that it is too much. The amount of sleep necessary is apparently regulated by a number of different circumstances. One of the elements involved is the soundness of sleep—some people sleep lightly; others, heavily. Sleep may also vary from night to night in the life of a particular individual, being affected by temperature, noise, climate, food, and other such factors. It is observable that the young generally require more sleep than those of older years. The aged frequently flourish on comparatively little sleep, but may require more rest. Thus we find a clear division gradually arising between rest and sleep. Rest is very largely a process of reducing the exhaustion of resources without necessarily sacrificing consciousness. Sleep represents a more or less complete exclusion of the consciousness factor.

Some can sleep more easily in the early morning hours. Many artists and creative persons find that they work best in the deep hours of the night, and we wonder how this can be true if the night energies have a tendency to benumb or lower the vibratory rate. I think the answer is that these creative geniuses are, for the most part, sedentary persons. They are therefore inclined to achieve a kind of physical relaxation in which they rest the body, but are able to maintain the stimulation of the mind. Also, as the person's internal life strengthens, he becomes less and less dependent upon the patterns of external living. The person who is psychologically in nearly constant communion with his inner life, requires a different kind of rest and a different kind of energy than the person whose objectives are almost totally physical. Therefore, the scholar, the artist, the mystic, the poet will often find their inspiration at night, when the rest of the world slows down and the interruption, discord, and pressure of daily activities disappear. The individual's own creativity is most likely to be available to him in quiet composure, where he achieves a kind of vision, a kind of sleep experience without actually being unconscious. He has made a more or less conscious bridge between himself as an objective person and his own subjective psychic resources. If he were under tremendous nerve stress, fatigue would probably put him to sleep, but if he is relaxed, he is able to be receptive to the psychic impulses which most of us record only in dream phenomena.

The most important and vital dreams that come to the individual do not come in the period of deepest sleep. The intensity or soundness of sleep gradually decreases. Normally, the person sleeps the most completely and heavily immediately after going to sleep. Gradually, over a period of hours, the sleep intensity diminishes, so that under normal conditions, the awakening is more gradual than the process of going to sleep. Thus, dreams are not as likely to arise in the first four hours of sleep as they are toward morning or toward the time of awakening. Not long prior to the point in which objectivity is restored by awakening, the sleeper passes into a condition between sleeping and waking which may be likened to a trance or deep meditation. He is not awake, but he is not completely asleep. The person often has the sense of being awake, though still asleep, and experiences a combination of pressures. It is at this time that dreams, visions, and premonitions are most vivid and most frequent. Being somewhat awake, the individual is able to remember the dream; being somewhat asleep, he is able to have it. And because he is partly aware objectively, he is able to contribute to the acceptance of the dream.

From what we have been able to learn, I would assume that the pro-dromic dream, or the dream that has to do with the condition of the individual in some stressful situation, will usually break through at this time, because after all, the pressureful dream seeks to be remembered. Nature wants us to know that dream when we wake up, because if we are unaware of it, then it cannot serve us objectively. So the problem of the dream bringing with it an awareness of its own meaning or purpose is met by nature providing a peculiar relationship of sleeping and waking to serve as the medium for this dream.

In this mysterious middle distance between true sleep and waking, there is a period in which the two zones of consciousness seem very close together. The Egyptians were aware of this—as were most ancient peoples—and they declared that it was in these small hours of the morning that the two worlds, the visible and the invisible, were the closest together. They believed that this was the reason why births and deaths are most numerous at that time. For in these hours, situations come to such a fine edge that the two states of existence seem to mingle and move together and flow into one, and then gradually, as the hours proceed, separate again, with man returning to an objective or exterior consciousness.

This peculiar psychological process occurs during the period of twilight, and the twilight hour corresponds with a kind of equilibrium between the earth energy and the solar energy. The first ray of the solar light is returning. It exists as an auroral glow, reflected in the sky from some other part of the heaven where day has already arrived. It is, however, merely a glow of anticipatory light; and in the process of the mingling of this first feebleness of the solar energy with the subtle energy of the earth, there comes a brief time when these two energies are brought into equilibrium. As night falls, the earth conquers the solar energy; as dawn comes, the solar energy conquers the earth. The sun-god, Horus, slays Python, the god of night. But in the period of equilibrium, there is a mysterious foreshadowing, or symbolic statement, of equilibrium in the psychic life of man. For the moment, there is no conflict. Things are in such complete balance that both of the areas of activity are in harmony, each with the other. And it is in this peculiar suspension that man has the greatest availability of his total life. In these moments, he is not dominated by the external, nor is he submerged in the internal, for each has united with the other.

The Egyptians therefore symbolized the twilight of the dawn as a door between two worlds—an entranceway or gate in which lives could move both ways. In these hours, according to the Hermetic doctrine, the Psychopompos, or Herder of Souls, herds souls back and forth between the world of the dead and the world of the living, or between the world of sleeping and the world of waking. And in those moments when the two conditions of energy come into equilibrium, they form a mysterious alchemical compound. Perhaps it is the ancient symbol of the marriage of the sun and moon, as the symbol of the marriage of spirit and matter. Here, in this equilibrium, there is a moment of validity that never occurs at any other part of the twenty-four hours of the day. The old peoples believed that this point of equilibrium lasted only for a few minutes—perhaps only about three minutes—before the solar energy begins to gain ascendancy.

Now, why is this not also true in the evening hours? Why is not the twilight between light and darkness equally important? The answer is that the nerve stress of the day has produced a psychic exhaustion, and because of this, the psychic equilibrium is not achieved. The condition seems to be based partly upon the body having first attained rest. Consequently, it is in the morning hours, and not in the evening hours, that this peculiar transitional period exists. It is usually somewhere between four and five a.m., differing with the seasons and the ancient system of planetary hours, and being conditioned to some degree by the motions and positions of the heavens each day at that hour.

In this peculiar suspension, then, it seems as though the entire person is open at one time. Now actually, man does not have the conscious experience of this openness, but he does awaken energized, with more abundant self-control, with greater optimism for the day, with stimulation to make plans come true. He arises, if he is in good health, with the proverbial bounce—and then proceeds immediately to waste half of it with his setting up exercises. By the time he gets through with those, he is ready to go back to bed again. But he feels good about it, and he is optimistic, and that is a very important factor. Incidentally, we will never find an animal doing setting up exercises. But a lot of people believe it helps, and the belief will help them, if the exercises do not. Socrates pointed out once that exercise was meaningless unless the individual who was exercising was accomplishing something. He absolutely refused to take a walk unless he was going somewhere; but he strongly recommended that everyone be going somewhere.

At any rate, this psychology of awakening also gives us a key to these twilight experiences in the morning hours. If it is true—and there seems much to sustain this—that there is a peculiar psycho-chemical balance, and that two states of consciousness have the greatest possibility of mingling without conflict at that time, then it is obvious that the internal life of man is most available to him in these hours; also, that the consciousness will then have the greatest receptivity to knowledge. Thus, if man has any ability to explore himself, he will have the greatest facility in doing this in these particular periods of time. Having at that moment the greatest availability of his own totality, he is then perhaps as wise as he can ever be in this world. The Egyptians also had the thought that it is not important whether man remembers these things or not; that actually, a certain internal psychic balance is maintained by this interchange during the mysterious twilight hour, whether we know it or not; and that this interchange is very important in maintaining the psychic health of the person. If he does not know anything about it, this is perfectly all right; but he does arise with clearer mind and with greater available intuitive power because of this experience.

It follows, then, that if there is a need for some particular exchange of basic idea or energy, we are very likely to have the significant dream experience in this particular time of the meeting of the two natures. This is the time when the psychic nature can most directly communicate with the objective functions of the body and mind. It is at this time that the will of Heaven can be most quickly known on earth. It is at this moment that the Divine establishes its relationship to the person in every single twenty-four-hour period. This is something that perhaps needs to be remembered, for it is a kind of daily psychic quickening, a process of re-establishing a covenant between the inner man and the outer personality. This covenant is necessary to life, and if a situation in the conduct of an individual or in his habits becomes so impossible that this covenant cannot be established, then he is in trouble.

Now, we may say, "What of a person who is in some occupation where he has to work on the 'graveyard shift,' so that he has to be awake during these hours?" Research into the problem seems to point out that under those conditions, the exchange still takes place, but it is less obvious to the person. After all, the procedure is exceedingly rapid, and just as it can occur without any apparent interruption of sleep, so it can occur without apparent interference with conscious activity. In fact, there is even a recorded case of a man who could sleep without inter-ruption of conscious activity. This person was shot in the brain during World War I, and did not sleep again for eighteen years. He worked three shifts a day, twenty-four hours a day, without being tired, and was never aware of sleeping; but actually, he was sleeping most of the time, but doing so in a series of sleep experiences lasting only fractions of a second. He was having constantly alternating consciousness and uncon-sciousness, but it was so rapid that he was not aware of it. Nature takes care of these things unless we prevent her from doing so.

Thus, there is much to indicate that this psychic experience does normally take place, even though it may not always be known to the person, and that it is vibratorily necessary to man. It would seem, also, that this peculiar twilight dawn is the great period of the instruction of man. Whereas in the rest of the day he is instructed by the world around him, in this period he is instructed by the world within him and behind him. And as a result of this instruction, there is a constant flowing of intuitive truth into his consciousness, which is the basis of certain growth within himself. Man must be moved not only by the circumstances around him, but by the life within him; and as the life within him has very little authority during his waking hours, it is in this other period that the inner life has its moment of authority. This moment provides the tremendous energy release that protects the individual not only for the rest of the twenty-four hours, but perhaps for many days. This peculiar psychological process may in due time earn a place in modern psychological research.

Today we are not inclined to think of the dreamer's world as anything more than perhaps an area of psychological function in which the individual releases, through the relaxation of his objective faculties, his own interior subconscious content. There may, however, be a valid concept underlying the idea that if sleep represents a gradual retiring into the subjectivity of our own inner life, there may be locked within this inner life a great deal more than psychology as yet has been willing to admit.

PART III.

SELF-INSTRUCTION THROUGH DREAMS

The oracular procedures of the Greeks could not have succeeded, had the oracles of the Pythian Apollo at Delphi not been for the most part true. It is, of course, certain—and this is the out for the modern skeptic—that these oracles were often ambiguous, difficult of interpretation, and obscure until the events actually transpired. Gathering a record of these reports, however, Cicero came to the conclusion that the majority of them were wise beyond the wisdom of the world; that there was something about them that transcended the judgment of conscious man. And in many instances, they were amazingly fulfilled to the smallest detail. Undoubtedly, the reason the Greek oracles were famous and were consulted by persons in every class of life, was the reputation they gradually gained for accuracy. This has also been mentioned by older writers. Even the most grudging have admitted that these oracles were universally constructive; that their recommendations were for the private and public good; that they did contribute a great deal to peace of mind and the guidance of states and leaders. Many of their less fortunate revelations also proved to be true—their warnings were seldom ignored without disaster.

Even Socrates seems to have admired the oracles, and to have acknowledged that they represented perhaps one of the deepest sources of man's possible knowledge of life and the world. Many of the oracles were broadly informative. They brought answers to questions in art, science, religion, and philosophy; they assisted in the preservation of crops; they aided the agriculturist in his plans for the harvest; they warned of storms and of pestilences. It was rather obvious to the ancients that such information was not normally to be attained in a waking state.

Now, the priestesses of Delphi, who were selected with the greatest care, were usually young women, although some reached older years with great dignity and distinction. These individuals were not trained in the worldly pursuits. They were virgins of the temple, living apart and alone in a cloistered existence. They were not instructed in statecraft or in medicine or in any of these subjects, but were assured that the truthfulness of their revelations depended upon the purity and integrity of their own lives. This, I think, is a further point of interest, and one that will bear consideration.

Obviously, the normal state of man can be both naturally and artificially deranged. Among most older peoples, the insane, those hopelessly infirm of mind, were regarded with a peculiar veneration. They were believed to be very close to God; they were God's own. They did not belong really in this world, and it was the responsibility of all to treat them with kindness, and to protect them, sometimes even from themselves. Their madness was considered as something like the divine madness of the Dionysiac cult induced by the juice of the vine—an intoxication that was held, in religious ritual, to open the mysterious interior perceptions, so that the individual seemed to suddenly escape from his human limitations and be able to commune with powers beyond this world.

Many of the early American Indian tribes also made use of this broad concept. With them, trances were usually brought on either by hypnotic means or by a form of auto-suggestion. The old medicine priests seem to have been able to cast themselves into trances more or less at will. And in tribal life, they had an unusual opportunity to demonstrate the accuracy of their foreknowledge. They were depended upon in a time when no dependable sciences existed, when laws and codes did very little to protect either the individual or the group. The person who had no rights, no privileges of legal or medical help, who was without any advantages of modern psychology or classical philosophy, built his life very largely upon phenomena, and these phenomena were nearly always associated with the mystery of sleep and the power of the soul to depart in sleep to explore those things which it most needed to know.

Out of this thinking, whether it be held to be mystical or psychological, we have come to certain practical conclusions that affect the practice of modern psychology and psychiatry to a marked degree. One of the conclusions is that in many instances, sleep phenomena are a valuable aid in the interpretation of the psychic complex of the human personality. Under certain conditions, dreams are not only keys to characteristics, but do constitute a form of admonition, a warning, or an inclination—a kind of instruction by which nature would seek to assist us in the immediate understanding of some peculiarity of our own emotions or thoughts. We know that everywhere nature eternally strives to repair the damage that is caused by human ignorance. If this damage is too great, nature is not equal to the task; but wherever possible, nature sets into action auto-corrective mechanisms to assist us in restoring the equilibrium upon which normalcy and health depend.

Many interesting experiences relating to this type of helpfulness by nature have been recorded. An individual, even without sleep, will suddenly become acutely aware of some deficiency in his own nature. He will have a flash of insight that forms a corrective pattern to deliver him from some emergency in which he is in danger of becoming involved. There are many instances of foreknowledge of this kind, cases where persons have canceled a trip on a train which was afterwards wrecked, or have decided not to take a certain plane trip and the plane came to disaster. This kind of fore-warning, or premonition, we know because it is testified to by generations of sincere and thoughtful persons.

Most of these warnings, however, pass unheeded. We rationalize ourselves out of them. There are numbers of recorded cases, also, where persons have come to grief as a result of ignoring some kind of intuitional flash that might have saved them. In our daily way of existence, we do not take it for granted that this internal insight is legitimate. We do not feel impelled to follow it. If it does not fit into our preconceptions, we ignore it. If it is inconvenient to follow its instructions, we violate them, and have certain argumentative procedures by which we justify our attitude. This is particularly true in the case of conscience, where we do experience certain very strong pressures which sometimes are accepted and recognized, but often violated. We have no full explanation of the conscience process, but we are inclined to feel that what we call conscience has to do with the individual's violating some preconception upon which he has learned to lean, or the validity of which he has accepted. Therefore, conscience does not represent any spiritualized faculty, but merely the voice of his traditional acceptances. Psychology, however, does recognize the fact that violations of the conscience mechanisms will nearly always prove detrimental. They destroy a degree of integration within the person, causing him to lose respect for himself. If he feels he is transgressing some value that he holds to be real, he is disappointed in himself, and he also develops the fear mechanism, because he subconsciously feels that he is opening himself to some kind of retribution.

Now, conscience operates when we are awake, but we have every reason to suspect that it operates even more actively when we are asleep; for nearly all impulses and instincts are more powerful when the conscious mind does not modify their pressures. The conscious mind of man causes a focalizing of objective awareness. The individual becomes acutely centered in his objective nature, and is therefore exceptionally responsive to the visible and physical things around him, and less responsive to the invisible, superphysical things within him.

The question may be asked—does man know more when he is asleep than when he is awake? I would say that he probably does not know more, but that he is more aware of what he knows. In the waking state, the individual does not have immediate access to the various levels of his own subconscious. In other words, he cannot be consciously aware of the subconscious. About the only part of his internal defense mechanism that is available to him is memory. Memory can and does issue warnings, but the individual frequently resists memory on the ground that each new situation is a unique thing, and therefore cannot be explained merely by reference to previous experiences. Thus, the burglar who has been jailed twice, may remember this, but it will not prevent him from making a third attempt, because he will feel that he now has worked out the perfect crime. Later he will remember that this did not work either, but by that time, he will be planning on a new course of procedure that he believes will violate his expectancies of being caught.

Thus memory does not serve us in everything, but it makes available a small part of our own previous experience. A very great part of that general experience, however, is not remememberable by any conscious process, and therefore, only certain phases of our own dispositions can be reached by the memory technique. On the level of the unremembered, there may also be a great deal that is truly known, but that we do not know that we know. This, in turn, causes a series of experiences which occasionally come into our objective understanding. Here again, we have inspirational moments—sudden mystical stretches or instances of insight. Something totally beyond the ordinary, which memory alone will not explain by normal procedure, is suddenly known to us.

In this "sudden-knowing" process, I believe there is another element that we have to bear in mind, which may have an effect upon the entire problem of learning from dreaming. Man's inner life is undoubtedly archetypal, and by that I mean that it represents a pattern. Man's internal organization is built upon a lawful formula, and depends for its continuance upon obedience to basic laws of existence. Thus, inside himself, man is a law-abiding creature, even though in his outer personality, he may be a law-breaker. Mentally and emotionally, he seeks to outwit his own lawfulness. He finds innumerable excuses, and in the course of ages, the external condition of man has come to deviate markedly from his internal nature. The reason for this is that objectivity, by the intensity of its processes, has come to be regarded as the final reality, and the problems that arise around us have precedence over the pressures that arise within us.

If, therefore, as a result of tradition, heredity, indoctrination, and experience—with all of these to a measure misunderstood—we arrive at a certain conclusion or attitude, we may develop a total personality which is psychologically unsound. Yet this personality may not be so considered, either by the individual or by his associates, because he may live in a world in which this kind of unsoundness is prevalent. Since most people are like himself, he considers his own nature to be normal; and in this sense of normalcy, he goes on breaking rules and laws imposed by nature because others break them. Such laws as will bring with them immediate physical punishment, we are inclined to keep; but laws that affect us primarily on a psychic level, we neither understand nor appreciate, nor do we sense the need to obey them.

This means, substantially, that the inner life of man may not condone his outer conduct, be entirely sympathetic with it, or recognize it as a best way of action. To meet this situation, man builds more and more rational defenses. He tries to convince himself, he psychologizes himself, or permits himself to fall under the hypnosis of prevalent attitudes. Now, the hypnotized person must, to a measure, temporarily fulfill the wishes of the hypnotist. In the same way, a hypnotized society must fulfill the purposes or accepted procedures of that society. Once we assume the normalcy of a social pattern, this pattern begins to move in upon us and require our allegiance. Thus, we may build up two distinct levels of psychic entity, with the outer level almost entirely dependent upon outward circumstances. From this psychic level comes a kind of static drag. It causes the traditionalist, the person who resists change, the dogmatist, and the exclusionist. It leads to legislation to protect entrenchment rather than progress. And all through this procedure, everyone is doing what he believes to be right, but no one knows what right actually means.

Now, we can go along like this, making a very choice group of cultivated mistakes. We can go on breaking one natural law after another; and if our infringements are not too massive, we are very likely to drift through the years with only those general discomforts and inconveniences that we can blame on someone else. But actually, we are not living well; we are not being true to the rules of our own existence; we are betraying something within ourselves while we are trying to protect the surface of our consciousness. This situation frequently leads to the building up of pressures. The deviation of the personality from the inner integration of life may become more pronounced, and detrimental attitudes may take over. The individual may find himself inundated in his fears and worries. He may find his natural optimism ebbing away, and his health gradually deteriorating.

This situation can and often does result in a desperate effort on the part of the archetypal consciousness to reassert itself over the life of the individual. If a life is going outwardly contrary to its inward need, nature will not permit this disaster without making some effort to correct the situation. If there seems to be no way in which the person can receive the necessary instruction as the result of his own ability to interpret value, this instruction is pressed upon him from within himself in some symbolic form. Sometimes this pressure is so great that it breaks through even in the waking hours; but as the hours of sleep are nearly always available and represent a minimum of resistance on the part of this badly oriented personality, it is most common for these important recommendations to be thrust upon him in the form of dream symbols.

The subconscious cannot impress itself directly upon us because of its own nature, which is essentially formless. We cannot actually behold the face of integration. We do not know what it looks like. We do recognize, however, that it can be communicated, or in one way or another made somewhat evident to us, by means of symbols. Actually, we cannot understand any abstraction unless it is clothed or put into a likeness that is comprehensible. It is impossible for us to draw a picture of virtue. The only way we can understand it is by means of examples, and examples are a form of symbolism. We use the example to indicate the principle; even a formula remains comparatively meaningless until an example is provided. So in our dream or thought process, any important message must be conveyed to us by means of material supplied by our own psyche in such a way that it will be meaningful to the objective personality. Therefore, the symbolism used must be derived from the objective world.

Assuming that this subjective conscious is a kind of ancient teacher or sage, let us imagine for a moment what our reaction would be if some such person should suddenly enter into our physical way of life. Suppose some very wise person made himself available to the needs of a very foolish man. The chances are that the entire procedure would be utterly non-productive. The wise man would not be accepted by the foolish man. He would be told that the qualities he is trying to teach are old-fashioned and no longer applicable. Thus, the direct admonitional procedure would be of very little value, unless it were accompanied by something that sets it apart from common experience, and in which something stronger than words becomes the basis of the communication of ideas. Sometimes, therefore, the archetypal image will impress itself in the form of a vision, in which a person, usually a celestial or sublime being, suddenly appears as though in actual reality, communicates the instruction, or gives the warning or the admonition, and then vanishes back into the mysterious, abstract regions from which it came.

The impact of such an experience—visual and auditory—upon the lower personality is much more profound by the very mystery with which it is involved. Such a visitation, so-called, could not be taken lightly, and the course of history has frequently been changed by visions of this kind. Yet the admonition given in the vision was not something entirely unknown to the person who received it. It was an admonition subconsciously known, internally recognized to be true, but ignored or willfully forgotten by the ambitious person who did not wish to be limited by the dictates of his own conscience. Thus, the question as to whether this type of visitation represents the addition of knowledge or merely the revelation of the knowledge—a new degree of impression from that which is eternally true—this is a situation of psychological significance.

There is another point that I think is interesting in connection with this—namely, the so-called warning or instructive admonition. We know perfectly well that a truly enlightened person, or some impartial machine, which impersonally accepted all the factors of our personality into an equation, could theoretically give us a fairly concise statement of our probabilities in a given situation. Also, we know that if we had the wisdom and could foresee things that would likely arise—we could avoid difficulties that are practically inevitable because of the course we are following. Yet these things are not evident to us in our normal state. Thus, the admonitional or instructive vision or dream does not necessarily mean that a foreign or outside entity is instructing us. It can well mean that a deeper and better part of ourselves is providing us with a larger measure of insight into the probabilities of our own conduct than would be objectively possible. And because the universe is lawful, and because all conduct must have its consequences, there are many phases of prophecy which only represent recognition of cause and effect and their inevitable operations.

These things cause us to have certain forebodings which may make us change our conduct, or rescue ourselves from the danger of too heavy a debt, or prevent ourselves from making an unreasonable alliance. There are cases in which a person planning to enter into partnership with another individual has had a strong premonitional dream not to do so. Now, does this mean that a guardian angel intervened at the proper moment? More likely, the truth lies in the fact that man, as a psychic entity, is capable of a greater skill in the estimating of character than is possible to his objective consciousness. The inner consciousness of the individual sees more, understands better, observes more acutely, than the external consciousness. And whereas the personality focus can be deceived by appearances, the inner part of man is not so easily deceived.

This does not necessarily mean that this inner consciousness is infallible, but it does usually mean that it is superior to the objective consciousness in the quality of its testimonies. There are undoubtedly instances in which intuition has been wrong, in which so-called insight has been incorrect, and where even a powerful mystical experience has not resulted in the end that was presumed to be inevitable. But it is also certain that millions of persons have been protected from themselves by this type of insight, and have been wonderfully guarded when it appeared that otherwise they would have fallen into the most cruel dilemmas.

The dream most commonly experienced has to do with the individual's integration. Nearly always, when a person is under pressure, when situations around him are out of hand and bewilderment and fatigue set in, he is in very real need of some form of internal communication. He needs to find his own center, and to receive from this discovery a new vitality with which to cope with illusion, or with which to achieve victory over error when it appears to be closing in upon him. The usual problem, then, is to recognize the dream as a group of symbolical symptoms that have to do with some phase of character or temperament. These symptoms most frequently express themselves as the result of a critical alignment of problem factors. Very often they will precede a crisis, and if they are not in some way regarded, the individual from then on falls immediately into a more desperate situation.

The symbols used in such dreams are derived from a kind of vocabulary of natural figures—natural objects that have certain interpretive overtones, objects with which we particularly associate values. These values arise from our mythology, legendry, lore, art, literature, or culture. The subjective nature moves as far toward the concrete as possible, and the objective nature must reach as far as it can into the subjective, toward the abstract, to meet this impression pattern that is seeking to come through. And if we are fortunate, there is a meeting of these two, forming a bridge for the actual communication of the instruction, whatever it may be. It is quite proper and right to say, therefore, that man does receive a kind of instruction from his dreams. If he does not take advantage of this right and privilege he has in nature, then the fault lies largely with himself, and not with nature's intention.

If man, from the early part of his culture, had accepted the meaning of his dreams and their symbols more generally and more generously, the chances are that there would be less need for psychologists today. Each individual could interpret his own inner life. But because we have relegated most symbolism to a mythological and imaginary sphere, we have forgotten that symbolism is a continuing language, and that the ancient myths and legends are still the fabric for the communication of subjective impulse. We no longer literally accept myths, but the myths themselves continue to form this alphabet of meaningful symbols for the communication of internal impulse.

Now, the symbolic message given in a dream always bears a direct relationship to the personal need. And just as persons interpret myths and legends differently, so that even mythologists have no common mind on these things, so it is true that symbols have different meanings to different persons and at different times. But always, there is *a* meaning, and that meaning is in some way related to the individual's own personal psychological pattern. In trying to estimate meaning, therefore, it is wise for the individual to ask himself certain questions: "What does this mean to me now? Why did it happen to me just at this time? What does it tell me that I should know in order to prevent the fulfillment of the negative aspects of the dream itself?" If the dream is morbid, it indicates that there is a negative factor at work in life. Therefore, this factor must be found and corrected. If the person does not find the meaning, refuses to accept it, or misinterprets it, the dream is likely to be repeated. When the problem is corrected, the dream has served its purpose, and will cease.

The time of awakening from a dream is sometimes of the greatest significance, inasmuch as it generally tells one of two things. Waking up either indicates acceptance, and the reduction of tension by acceptance brings the psychological intensity of the dream to its natural termination; or the waking up may indicate that there is so much resistance to the message of the dream that at a certain point, the individual rejects the experience completely and escapes by waking up. Under analysis, therefore, the same dream may recur, but as various phases of the analysis proceed, the individual will awaken at a different part of the dream. When this happens, it is an indication of certain acceptances or massive rejections on the part of the dreamer.

Now, while the instructional dream does always relate to the problem or need of the individual, this relationship is not always directly evident. The dream may be a moving dream—going forward, or upward, or from now downward, but it summarizes in one way or another, the nature of the confusion in ourselves and its true and often unrecognized cause. And here we come, perhaps, to one of the keynotes of the entire situation. Things have several apparent causes and one true cause. The attitudes we hold, the situations that arise in our lives, are nearly always related to some basic principle, or to some basic factor with which we have been unable to cope successfully. Most persons' lives are projections of a small group of psychic patterns. These patterns may be traceable to early life—perhaps to an accumulation of habits; perhaps to certain strong ambitions or desires. Whatever may be the causes, there are nearly always a few basic pressures that have become submerged and make themselves known only by a series of scattered and sometimes apparently unrelated circumstances.

One of the most common examples of this type of thing is multiple marriage. If an individual makes an unfortunate marriage, there is nothing extraordinary about it—this may happen to nearly anyone. But if he makes another similar unfortunate marriage, and perhaps three or four such marriages during a lifetime, there is almost always a basic cause in the individual himself. Another person may be in perpetual business difficulties. I know of one individual who had this type of problem. He would try very hard, he would build a good business, and things would apparently go well. Then at the critical moment, he would suddenly lose all interest in his work. About that time, of course, a competitor would take over. This happened to him a dozen times. It resulted in a broken home, and it added continuously to his difficulties, to the point where he became so disturbed that he was contemplating suicide; there seemed to be no way out of this recurrent difficulty.

Things of this nature cannot be considered merely as separate circumstances. Where there is a basic temperamental intensity that is causing trouble, there may be a number of excuses, but there has to be one true cause. The chronic worrier, the individual who is by nature critical or domineering, or the person who is utterly and impossibly stubborn—these characteristics arise from something; and as long as they remain uncorrected, they will result in difficulty. The general thought used to be that if you have a bad disposition, get over it. To a measure, this is still good advice, but it has its limitations. If the cause of the trouble is deeper than the dispositional peculiarity, and we merely inhibit the peculiarity by imposing will upon it, then the major difficulty will probably break out elsewhere. Thus, the individual who fought desperately to overcome a bad temper finally controlled the temper, but he became an alcoholic in the process. The problem was never solved.

The value of the dream as an instruction factor is that it is frequently possible, by means of dream analysis, to penetrate into this area of essential cause. We are able to reach symbolically into the thing itself—that which is properly and eternally to blame; the thing is real. For one individual whom I knew, this symbolism came in the form of a dream of the Jack and the Beanstalk story.

This person was a timid soul, whose intellectual achievements were rather good, but whose economic status was always hazarded by lack of personality drive—he simply could not advance his own cause. He suffered from a terrible inferiority complex, and this led him to continually underestimate himself and to be a considerable disappointment to those around him. He did not dream a great deal—in fact, very seldom—but under a process of analysis, he began to have a certain dream, and this dream was nothing more or less than the familiar story of "Jack and the Beanstalk." Now, for him this might seem to be little more help than his previous unawareness of the situation, but the story of Jack and the Beanstalk has considerable psychological meaning.

As the dream proceeded, it became evident that there was an ogre-factor in the life of this individual—an ogre that terrified him and caused him to feel that he had to hide. And this, of course, tied into his timidity. Now, it might be quite easy to say that this ogre could be a person; that it might have been an overly stern or dominating parent, or a cruel guardian. It might also represent some basic fear, or some form of guilt mechanism, by which the individual tormented himself. It could be a moral problem in his life which had never been sublimated or clarified.

In this particular instance, the ogre represented a rather neutral thing in comparison to the intensity of the pattern. The individual was an adopted child, and before adoption, had been in a public institution for several years. The institution was the ogre, and it carried with it certain other factors. First of all, as far as he was able to learn, he was illegitimate, and had been left in this institution, deserted, by his parents. The institution itself had not been especially cruel to him; he had only been one of many unfortunate children who had to be cared for, but to whose inner life very little thought was given. Finally, adoption brought a certain fulfillment of a better way of life, but the institution and the circumstances involved with it became a gigantic shadow for him. It was the shadow of a forlornness in the beginning of life, of a world first experienced as a strangely heartless thing—not cruel, but simply without heart.

To this man, the world gradually became the extension of the orphanage; and everything in the world that happened to him became an extension of this cruel message that had reached him in early life, and had stamped him with a peculiar mark of being an outcast. To make the matter even more complicated, this man, trying to fight this thing inside himself, had completely submerged it. He had told no one. It was only after analysis began that he even admitted that he had ever been in an orphanage. And it was only after a long period of work with a counselor, that he finally admitted his illegitimacy.

All these factors combined with the sensitivity of his own nature to produce this ogre kind of dream. Somehow he knew the story, and he related both the relevant and the irrelevant parts. He went through the early part of the dream without any particular emotional involvement, but when he came into the house where the ogre was, he became completely paralyzed with fear—fear that the world would know this awful secret that he had carried throughout his life. It was a very sad, almost ridiculous situation; yet it had eaten deeply into the life of this individual.

After considerable counseling, the ogre dream was finally overcome, and not in the way that might be expected, where the ogre disappeared or where Jack was able to cut down the beanstalk, as in the original story, and the ogre and everything perished together. In this case, there was a gradual transformation of the ogre, until the dreamer and the ogre became quite compatible, and they were getting along excellently at the last report. He had completely overcome the fear.

Another type of dream that is based on folklore or legendry is what we might term the *Amfortis dream*. In the Grail legend, Amfortis, the King of the Grail, attempted to rescue the holy spear from the black magician; but the black magician turned the spear and thrust it into the side of Amfortis. Amfortis had intended to use the spear to destroy the power of evil; but the power of evil took hold of the spear and wounded the King of the Grail, and this wound would not heal. So the Amfortis type of dream symbolizes some ill that will not get well. A common form of this dream is the eternal toothache. There are cases where a person has dreamed month after month of having a toothache. Others dream of being crippled, having some deformity that by its very nature will not get well.

This type of dream seems to indicate a certain kind of psychological problem to which the person has associated an inevitability. He has convinced himself that this condition will not change, and this conviction usually involves some kind of loyalty. He may feel obligated, either by circumstances or selfobligation, to a way of life or to a situation that is gradually becoming unendurable. This kind of dream has also been associated with a loss from which the person never expects to be able to recover. A man in his early sixties, through unwise or unreasonable investments, lost most of his financial holdings. This resulted in a dream of not getting well, because the man consciously believed that he was in a hopeless condition of financial sickness. There are cases in which married persons who are unable to maintain compatibility, but whose religion forbids divorce, develop this dream of not getting well.

These dreams are instructive. Their purpose is not to tell the person that he cannot get well, but to point out to him that his condition is due to a pattern. Sometimes the whole mystery is solved the moment the dream is presented and analyzed. It is then necessary to point out that this condition is not due to the fact that he cannot get well, but to the fact that he has no ego in this area. Psychologically, he has drained off his resources so that he can no longer energize any activity—the energy is flowing away from him in the blood of his wound. But the wound can be healed the moment the person realizes that it originates in a complex, a pattern which has gradually become a reality to him through its symptoms. And just as the dream gives one group of symbols for the interpretation of the situation, so the circumstances through which the person has passed form another group of symbols bearing on the original cause.

Once the individual comes face to face with this cause, he can begin to work with it. And he discovers the degree to which he has succeeded by the gradual transformation of the dream content itself. Finally, whatever the adversary is, becomes apparent; whatever the difficulty is, heals; and in some mysterious way, the wound is cured even though there was no expectation that it could be. Under therapy, the dream generally continues, but undergoes changes. When it is no longer dangerous or tragic or restraining, it is reasonably certain that the basic cause of the attitude has been reached and corrected. From this point on, the secondary symptoms fall away of themselves, for they cannot exist apart from the cause. Thus, the dream reveals the cause and also helps us to discover the degree of remedy that we have achieved. In this way, and in many other ways, the dream is a very instructive experience.

PART IV:
AN ALPHABET OF DREAM SYMBOLS

From the beginning of the study of dream phenomena, it has been observed that the dream is composed very largely of symbols. Gradually, it has come to be assumed, therefore, that a study of symbolism is one of the most simple and direct ways of approaching the interpretation of dreams. Symbolism itself has been so long a part of man's cultural heritage, that it may be regarded as one of his oldest and deepest traditions. It has been asociated with life since man began to speculate upon his own origin or the origin of other things, and among most peoples, the subject has developed into a highly organized legendry or lore, and also into a strong moral-ethical conviction. Some of the medieval thinkers took the attitude that all appearances, all things visible, are symbols of things invisible, and that we must therefore examine the whole universe in terms of symbolism if we ever hope to understand the operations of Universal Law. This Law, which is in itself formless, manifests its will, or its way, through an infinite diversity of forms, which are meaningful, purposeful, and are in some way extension of principles. These conclusions, which have been broadly accepted, provide man with a useful instrument for the interpretation of his own thinking.

The symbol descends to the average person through tradition. Whether we realize it or not, we are not only constantly confronted with symbolism in our daily living, but it has come into our consciousness through our associations, our reading, our religion, our arts and sciences, and through practically every specialized agency of cultivation. Those in various walks of life have developed intense symbolisms around familiar things—as the agriculturist, or the mechanic, or the metal worker. To the physician, the world is a series of symbols originating in the great processes of biology and physics. Disease manifests itself through symptoms, and a symptom is a symbol manifesting itself through a process, or through a moving circumstance in the structure of the individual. An extensive symbolism has also developed around the creatures of nature—animals, birds, fishes, insects.*

*For additional material on this subject, see: "Animal Symbolism in Religion and Art," by Manly P. Hall, in *The PRS Journal,* Vol. 20, #2-4 and Vol. 21, #1, (Autumn 1960 through Summer 1961 issues).

Even our ordinary use of words is rich with symbolism. Here the dictionary is a valuable aid, because nearly all words have two meanings—one a strict meaning, and the other a meaning by extension. The strict meaning may not be so useful, but the meaning by extension is itself little less than a dream interpretation. Wherever words move into symbolic usage, they have come to be so accepted in our own consciousness. Take, for example, the word *stream*. By its most common and familiar meaning, we visualize a mountain stream, or a rivulet of water coming down from the hills. But in the dictionary, we will find that this word has come to convey a flowing of ideas, or a flowing of values, rather than simply a flowing of water. Or take the word *storm*. The strict meaning would involve natural phenomena, but we also think of storm now as a synonym of war, of the struggle of life, of a catastrophe in personal affairs. We have extended the meaning into symbolism, by binding the basic symbol with a series of related patterns and ideas. These relationships are important clues to the interpretation of dream symbols, because they arise through our own experience or through our own ability to relate things with a degree of similarity though by nature or substance different.

Now, what does a word do to us? A word can do one of several things. We may start with the most pronounced negative—a word can do nothing; that is one of its functions. If it does not mean something to us, it remains not only uninteresting, but perhaps unintelligible. Or a word may cause a word exchange in our own consciousness. Many people who think they are thinking are merely exchanging words with each other. The word of one person suggests a word to the other person, and this suggestion becomes a chain of related words. Everyone has a wonderful time, everyone feels that the other persons are very congenial, but in the end, no one knows anything more than he did before. This is where words are substituted for ideas, and by this substitution merely perpetuate themselves, but are not carriers for any real meaning.

Another thing that a word can do is to cause a meaning to rise in our consciousness. We grasp at the word, and the word becomes the symbol of an idea. We therefore release from our own natures, by association, our own meaning of that word, and it is because we have the power to remember meanings of words that we are able to converse with each other. Actually, therefore, words are not so important in themselves; they are important only because they cause us to recollect ideas, to have these ideas brought from some dark mysterious file of the memory and injected into an immediate situation. This process has its definite relationship to dream existence, because we dream for the reason that we have this availability of ideas.

Thus, by nature and by choice, man surrounds himself with various symbols, emblems, or devices—colors, sounds, forms. These, in their own ways, tell what he is and what he is not. They may also reveal the areas of tension or stress that are most dangerous for him. If we want to interpret man's sleep symbolism, we should therefore study with equal interest his waking preferences. The type of picture he finds congenial, the type of music he listens to, the arrangement and color harmonies of the furnishings of his home, his selection of a model of an automobile, the programs he chooses on television or radio—these things are all symbols of attitudes and processes taking place within his own consciousness. By the exercise of such selectivity in his daily life, he is constantly seeking to compensate for his deficiencies or to obscure them or to defend himself against them.

Now, just as the symbols from our waking activities are reflected in our dreams, so it is quite possible for dream symbolism to influence us in the waking state. It is a symptom of danger to the integration of character if dreams become too prominent in the individual's waking life. A person, for instance, whose day is overshadowed by a bad dream, and who may require several days to recover from that dream, and allows it to influence his conduct while awake—such a person is not in good condition psychologically. If he allows these tendencies to drift too far, he may find that the pressures of his subconscious take over in his conscious affairs. For example, if a person has a dream in which a neighbor is unfriendly, and because of this, does not speak to the neighbor for a week afterwards, this is not good. So unless a dream is supported by adequate evidence, it is not wise to allow it to be too influential. I have known cases where a person, having thus had a dream of someone else, and becoming very edgy and unfriendly in the presence of that other person as a result, has caused the other person to react in like manner. To the dreamer, of course, this apparently proved the truth of the dream; yet the symbolism of that dream may actually have had an entirely different meaning from what was obvious to him.

One of the first points we must make, therefore, in regard to dream interpretation, is to remind the individual that the majority of dreams are not to be interpreted literally. Of course, occasionally one will be found—particularly a prodromic dream, or one relating to health—in which the individual has a clear premonition of physical difficulty; and this type of dream may invite a medical checkup. For the most part, however, dreams are not to be regarded as literal. This is a sad mistake that most people make. In the last thirty or forty years, I have had probably several hundred letters from people who have had a dream that a continent is going to sink, or a city is to be destroyed, who hastened to warn everyone they could of the impending disaster. They were then, I hope, pleasantly disappointed when the city did not disappear or the continent did not sink, but they were not quite able to understand how they could have so clearly seen the catastrophe if it were not going to occur. The problem is that these people tried to assume that a dream has to be literal. Their thinking was perhaps based on the fact that they had read of prophetic dreams that were fulfilled. But the majority of disaster dreams are never fulfilled, for the simple reason that they were not intended to be regarded as literal stories of a disaster. The threat is of a different type, and the dreamer must learn to unravel and interpret the symbolism.

I would strongly recommend, therefore, that all dreams be considered symbolical, unless other testimonies of an extraordinary nature are present. The symbolic dream always has to be solved by an answer to the question, "What does this dream mean to me?" This is not an easy question to answer, but essentially it is easier for the person who is dreaming to answer it than for anyone else, because a dream is always a production arising from factors which cannot be generally known. Even though certain classifications are possible, all dreams have a certain direct individuality, and similar dreams by different persons may have different meanings. It is only reasonable to say, then, that the meaning of a dream should be most available to the dreamer himself. Therefore, the best chance of having an adequate interpretation is that the dreamer will have at his command a fair understanding of dream symbol factors in order that he may interpret his own experience.

The basic elements of dream symbolism are almost certainly derived from folklore and from the unusual but natural interpretations we give to things. These basic meanings are surprisingly simple, and although they can be presented in an extremely learned way, we will probably come as close to them in Grimm's Fairy Tales and Aesop's Fables as anywhere else. From the beginning of man's experience, he has formalized certain archetypal concepts in his own consciousness. He has related and inter-related the common factors of daily living. It is now quite possible that some of this information descends to man as part of his common heredity; that it is essentially in his own folk nature.

The basic concepts of symbolism also come to the individual from his environment. From early childhood, he is exposed to traditional symbolical meanings. He receives them in nursery rhymes, in Biblical stories, in the literature he reads at school, and in one way or another, the familiar symbolism of his culture is imparted to him throughout life. A point that is worth noting here is that homogeneous culture groups are observed to have a more intense common language of symbolism than heterogeneous groups. In a culture whose national, religious, and racial existence has developed from one unified thread, persons grow up in environments in which meanings are simple and clear and constant.

Where everyone has the same general social experience, there will be a larger common denominator of symbolism. This does not mean that there will be no deviations in this group, but it does mean that there will be more conformity than in a heterogeneous civilization.

Thus, dreams involve an element of folk tradition. Now, in our Western life, we have a very insecure traditional background. Our traditions, having been derived from many areas, have been seriously broken up, have been mingled and intermingled without very much continuity or reason, until today they constitute more or less of a hodge-podge. We have no clear traditional ethics or morality. We have no clear background in our myths and legends and folklore. We are not like the Greeks, whose religion and philosophy were very closely interrelated. We are not like the Chinese, who closed their doors to foreign nations and remained aloof for ages. Our alphabet of dream symbols is derived from innumerable conflicting cultures. In a sense, this enriches the fabric, but it also compounds the difficulty in bringing the essential symbolism within our conscious control.

All peoples, however, regardless of their areas, have certain symbols in common. The primary group of such common symbolism relates to natural forces, for in all parts of the world, nature is reasonably consistent. It is true that in some areas we have a temperate climate, and in others a torrid or frigid climate, and these factors may modify the symbolism. But all over the world, if a man falls into the water and cannot swim, he will drown; if he does not eat, he will be hungry; if he is tired, he goes to sleep. These are large common patterns to which we may turn for certain generalities, which must then be carefully specialized.

Nearly all symbols that arise in our consciousness are of one of three orders. The first is what might be termed the "helpful" symbol. This ranges in its meaning all the way from extraordinary protection, wisdom, guidance, and leadership, through the entire gamut of pleasurable things —things of good fortune, of opportune intervention, or of spiritual consolation. The helpful symbols may carry a solutional impact, enabling the individual to understand or to bear some necessary activity.

The second group of symbols may be called "mysterious and mischievous" symbols. In these, elements of fortune and misfortune are curiously mingled. This type of symbolism suggests the trickster, the jester, minor connivances, and perhaps minor persecutions due to moods or fancies rather than any deep-laid strategies. These symbols are amusing or annoying, or sometimes a compound of both.

Then we have what might be termed "malevolent" dream symbols, relating to danger, suffering, humiliation, or the frustration of purposes. These symbols often represent obstacles that stand between us and the ends we desire.

In most cases, the dreams themselves can also be classified under one of these three headings, and the interpretation of a particular symbol will, of course, depend very largely on the type of dream in which it occurs. For example, we may dream of water. Now, we may dream of a beautiful sea, and we are sitting on the shore enjoying the splendor of it, perhaps watching a sunset; or we may be sailing upon the sea in a safe ship. This is the sea as a friendly symbol. Or the sea may appear as the mischievous symbol, in which we are in a small boat, tossed about, and become seasick. Or we may find the sea dashing itself against the shore and covering us with spray and perhaps destroying a little castle we have built by the edge of the sand. Here we have the sea as a mischievous factor—not really doing us a great deal of harm, but unpleasant or annoying to a degree. Then we have the sea as danger—the great storm, the tidal wave, the terrible inundation. Or we find ourselves upon a sinking ship, cast upon the waters. The sea becomes something we have to fight in order to survive. Perhaps we are upon a life raft, struggling to prevent ourselves from drowning, with great waves breaking over us or beating us against the shore. This is the sea as danger. With nearly all symbols, such modifications are possible within the scope of the symbol itself.

Symbolic forms may also be combined in dreams to produce monstrosities—chimera of one kind or another, or non-existent creatures. The ancients believed that such symbols had great religious significance, but we are now inclined to think that they simply represent composite dream symbols. Such compound symbolism is somewhat more difficult to interpret than the simple patterns.

Another difficulty presents itself when the dream situation consists of kaleidoscopic and comparatively dim and uncertain symbols. There are chaotic dreams, in which there is nothing but fragmentation, where things do not take any reasonable patterns nor assume any forms for which we can find a meaningful interpretation. Obviously, the more clearly defined the incidents or symbols are, the more likely they are to be remembered after the dreamer awakens. And when the dream unfolds as an orderly sequence, it is usually regarded as more important.

It is interesting to note that when we dream about people, the faces are usually missing; we do not actually see these people in their clear and natural appearances. There is a certain vagueness about persons, whereas other objects may be extremely clear. Probably the reason we do not generally use persons in their proper forms as dream symbols is that we have already interpreted these persons into their symbolic equivalents in our own subconscious. There are cases where a person's face is clearly recognizable in a dream, but this usually involves a specialized type of dream intensity. Another exception is in dreaming of famous people, who are probably not known to us personally, but whose likeness has descended to us so clearly in tradition that we almost inevitably identify the person. The likenesses seen in such instances are usually traditional appearances derived from art or other familiar sources. In dreaming of Abraham Lincoln, for example, we would almost certainly have a strong symbolic likeness available to us. The same is true in certain religious dreams, where images of Christ and Mary and the angels may take on a very clear and definite form.

We can take almost anything we dream about, and build a symbolism around it according to our own understanding. It is almost like a basic word test in which we search for word association; but in this case, instead of seeking for similar words, we seek for related meaning. Let us take as an example a very old and common symbol, the rabbit. Now, what does a rabbit suggest to us? For one thing, it might bring to mind the idea of rapidity, or its power to jump. It might also suggest other habits. When a rabbit is cornered, unable to escape, it remains absolutely still in an effort to conceal its identity or location. Then, of course, we associate rabbits very largely with intense productivity. Rabbits multiply with amazing speed, being very successful in this form of mathematics. We also think of the rabbit as a timid creature. On a more personal level, it may be that the rabbit is meaningful to us because we had one as a childhood pet. Or we may realize that we have a friend who looks very much like a rabbit under certain conditions. The rabbit, therefore, suggests many overtones, and in a context of symbolism, the more we think about these overtones, the more likely we are to draw out of ourselves the reason why we had a dream involving a rabbit. The pressure in the dream would indicate that in some way, this symbolism is significant to us, and by quietly exploring this meaning through conscious association, we may be able to clarify the dream when we otherwise could not.

Let us begin to think now of various types of familiar symbols with which we have certain associations. The moment we think of birds or animals or flowers or trees, let us also think in terms of what these have held as traditional meanings. It is not surprising, however, to find considerable originality in our own interpretations, for these are the natural results of our own attitudes toward life.

Flowers afford a good example of levels of meaning, particularly because of their relationship with many of the important functions of life. Flowers can symbolize birth; they are associated with marriage; and then, of course, on the more melancholy side, flowers are associated with the funeral and with death. In Eastern thinking, flowers symbolize spiritual unfoldment. Thus we have a wide range of meaning in flower symbolism. Sometimes the key to the interpretation of flower symbolism in a dream comes to us automatically with the dream itself, or soon afterwards when we can relate it to some circumstance around us that might very well be the cause of such a dream. Then our only problem lies in determining our own attitude toward the circumstance as represented by the dream sequence.

Birds have to do with messages, travel, insight, guidance or leadership, and uplifting ideas. Because they inhabit an airy region, they are likely to be associated with the mind and with thoughts. Birds are symbolical of various attributes, deriving their meanings from their appearance to us, or by their involvement in our affairs. If, for example, we dream of an eagle, and this eagle flies off and invites us to follow him, this represents an invitation to a more courageous approach or quest for something that is valuable or needed, because this bird has become associated with courage. If, however, this bird turns upon us to hurt us, then we are in danger of developing the attributes of the talon and the claw and the beak—in other words, the bird of prey—by which our own inner life is likely to betray us.

The owl is well known as the symbol of wisdom. It also represents mystery and the search for hidden things; and very often, because of its association with the city of Athens, it is a symbol of philosophy. The raven, or the other talking birds, may signify intuitive experiences, or suggest that advice or needed information is likely to reach us, or has reached us, but we have not yet been able to interpret it.

Caged birds usually represent limitations upon our love, our thoughts, and our affections. Birds associated with water generally represent man's emotional life; birds of the air have to do largely with the mental life. The swan, of course, is one of the most ancient symbols of human mystical insight, and appears in this form constantly in Western symbolism. In the Japanese and Chinese symbolism, the mandarin duck, which never leaves its mate and never has more than one mate, signifies fidelity, and in the experiences of these people, its appearance in a dream would probably carry that meaning. The Oriental peoples also have high regard for the crane or the stork, which also has a considerable role in European thinking. This bird was the symbol of patience because it would stand quietly on one foot for hours, watching a little pool of water and waiting for lunch. Therefore, patience, quietude, relaxation, and watchful waiting are indicated by this particular creature.

The dragon represents one of the most complex symbols in man's experience. In China, it is a good symbol. In Western civilization, it is generally not a good symbol, although under some conditions, it may be benevolent. The reason it is good in China is probably that the Chinese mind has been so deeply involved in mysticism that the unconscious content has become a thing of benevolence. For Western man, the unconscious is a thing of danger. The dragon, as a space symbol, usually represents the mysterious total power lurking at the source of man—a power of which he is afraid, which he does not dare to express, and which he can scarcely hope to ever understand. Therefore, to slay the dragon, is to overcome the fear of the unknown. To harness or tame the dragon, is to transform or make use of the unknown for the advancement of man's purposes.

Another mythical creature in symbolism is the unicorn. This mysterious horse with a horn on its forehead usually represents transmutation. It may appear in dreams as a solution symbol, indicating that matters can be handled. It is a promise or announcement that the insight or circumstances required to solve the situation will appear to be recognized, in due course, by the dreamer.

Various characters and figures from the age of fable—such as harpies, sirens, mermaids, nymphs, and things of that nature—representing elementary forces, tend to indicate appetites or rudimentary emotions within man. They have to do with instincts and impulses. In dreams, most of these submundane forms represent urges to do things that are not easily explainable. To dream of falling under their influence is indicative of imagination or psychism dominating the life.

Animals, as other symbols, can be grouped into those that are friendly to man, dangerous to man, or can combine both attributes—and most animals do combine both attributes. In various cultures, however, some animals are regarded as more benevolent than others. Therefore, in this symbolism, the cultural background is important. In Asia, for example, the elephant has always been a symbol of wisdom, and is regarded as a fortunate symbol. Int he West, this is not so easily understood because our legendry and lore do not entirely support the symbolism. We do, however, tend to associate the elephant with erudition, thoughtfulness, and shrewdness of mind. We also associate it with mass, weight, and awkwardness. It becomes a symbol of imponderable difficulties.

If the elephant is friendly, kindly, helpful, and in service to man, then it may well represent the confused, comparatively ill-adjusted personality that is useful to man, but is a large problem. The elephant symbolizes heavy matters, weighty decisions, but it also suggests some kind of a thorough mental factor—the idea that the necessary decisions can be made; that the matters can be clarified by greater thoughtfulness. If the elephant is tame, the situation can be controlled. If, however, the elephant is a destroyer, then it becomes a symbol of the tyranny of the uncontrolled mind, of intellect as a corrupting or negating force. Any brilliant or powerful animal that is set upon destruction, usually represents either the intensity of emotion or the power of self-will and pride in their more devastating sense.

To be identified with a powerful animal, to have such an animal as an ally or servant, may well signify strong resources available to the individual. I know one case where a person had a powerful bear-like animal that accompanies him as a faithful friend in his dream. Then this bear was killed in the forest by a hunter who did not know to whom it belonged. The owner wept bitterly in his dream, and wished that the bear could come back to life. Actually, in later interpretation it was found that this bear represented the man's business. This was his instrument of control in society, his source of prestige, his means of attaining various ends. And the anxiety that caused the dream was the danger that this business would be undermined and ultimately destroyed by a competitor, the hunter.

This type of dream can be clearly understood only if we know that the man is under this pressure in his business. He might have gotten some idea, of course, from the old association of the bears and the bulls with the stock market. Such associations frequently arise, and cannot be at all overlooked. I know of a case in England where a man dreamed that he had his pocket picked by an old lady with one of those old-fashioned folding parasols, a black bonnet, and a taffeta dress and coat. She had a very motherly, kindly appearance, but was an absolute pick-pocket. The symbolism would be meaningless to us, but it was very meaningful to this man. He was out on a limb with his investments, and was in danger of losing his holdings. Naturally, he was greatly worried over this prospect. In his dream, he went back subconsciously to one of the most common symbols used in England for the stock exchange—"The Little Old Lady of Threadneedle Street." That was the name of the London stock exchange, and this was the little old lady who was picking his pocket. The symbolism arose from perfectly natural association, but without a little help, the man would probably not have consciously bridged the interval.

Continuing with animal symbolism, we find that nearly all domesticated animals represent friendship for man. The horse, for example, is a beast of burden for man; therefore, it is frequently a body symbol. One old Chinese philosopher made the analogy of the foolish man walking down the road carrying the donkey on his back instead of riding the animal, as a symbol of man being controlled by his body. By extension, also, the horse can represent career, or the vehicle that is taking the individual toward his goals. And if the horse is injured, it may indicate the interruption of purpose or the fear of such interruption.

Animals that are frequently around the home usually become symbols of persons or conditions in the home. Small children are often represented by young animals—more often than by young children. It is interesting that when we dream of children, it probably means something else, but when we dream of kittens and puppies, it probably means children. One of the peculiar qualities of dreams is their dislike to be literal. This seemingly would be too easy, and would not have permitted any particular glory to descend upon Dr. Freud. Things had to be more complicated. Actually, home situations are not as often represented by home, as we know or think of the term, as by some relationship of a friendly, jovial, or emotional nature with creatures, situations, or conditions. A mortgage or a heavy responsibility upon the home, for example, may take the form of fear or worry about clothing.

Clothing, by the way, plays quite an important part in dreams. It is more often a symbol of concealment than of adornment. If the clothes are not contemporary with the times, this may represent out-of-date attitudes. To see ourselves in poorly fashioned garments, is to have subconscious awareness of misgivings or shortcomings in ourselves. To appear suddenly without garments is to be afraid of exposure or to be in the midst of a situation that might cause embarrassment. The individual who finds his garments suddenly soiled or injured, and is trying desperately to clean them again, is one whose conscience is probably giving him trouble. He is trying to clean something out of his character or temperament, and his attitude toward it is affected by his fear that others will observe his difficulty; for clothing represents that part of himself that is observed by others. If, however, the dreamer senses a lack of cleanliness on his skin, then it is more likely to indicate that he is worried about his own personality in relationship to himself. Thus, layers of circumstances move inward toward the essential nature of the individual.

In dreams about elders, the older persons, if of a benign nature, usually represent experience. They symbolize the source of further knowledge, of leadership, guidance, help, or perfection. The individual who seeks wisdom and understanding, is most likely to have this imparted in dream patterns through old persons, whom he instinctively associates with experience. Such dreams may also imply that the individual needs to have a deeper insight into his own nature. He needs to listen more acutely to the experience lessons that have been given to him in life. So the voice of experience in dreams usually speaks through the elder, or the prelate, or some person in high office. Always, the experience pattern speaks down from a superior level of attainment of some nature.

Now, if this elder is a sorcerer, a trickster, a demon, or any form of a malevolent being, then this elder is not giving out the voice of experience, but is speaking to us out of the prejudicial level of our own psychic development. It is telling us about things we have built into consciousness that are wrong. Therefore, it is giving ill advice; it is telling us that we have already psychologically betrayed ourselves; that we are under the pressure of false values. Perhaps what we have thought of as an opportunity is only a temptation; what we believed to be a firm judgment, was really a prejudice; what we believed to be strength of character, was nothing but narrow-mindedness. Thus, when information is imparted by malevolent aged persons or beings, it usually means that our experiences have not profited us well, that we have not understood or applied principles as nature intended.

Young people, children, newborn babes in dreams have the meaning that they would symbolically suggest. The majority of persons in this world, consciously or unconsciously, invest their own future in their children. Whether they know it or not, they consider the child as the extension of themselves. In dreams, therefore, the child is often an extension of the person into the future. It may symbolize a new beginning or a new reaction to circumstances. And the child symbol is usually associated with some major hoped-for improvement of our condition. It is far more likely to represent a new life in us than to actually refer to children around us.

This symbolism can also relate to the child in ourselves, a creature that never dies regardless of our age in physical years. It can be both the child-likeness and the childishness. As the child-likeness, it is the purity, the innocence, the basic spiritual integrity of the person; but as childishness, it is immaturity, impractical thinking, perpetual adolescence, and the failure of the life to mature. The meaning is indicated by the way the child functions in the dream. If it is a beautiful child, a loving child, a child for whom we feel the most admirable emotion, then it probably does represent the child-likeness, or the hope of a better self with which we are involved. If the child is delinquent, hateful, discordant, a pain and sorrow to us in our dream, then it represents our childishness, or lack of maturity.

The loss of a child in a dream is usually an indication of the giving up of a hope or a project or an idea that is very dear to us. Again, it is the extension of ourselves into the future. It may also, however, merely symbolize that we have weakened our own resolution and have thus sacrificed the child. The effort to save a child from disaster usually indicates that we are trying to save a value in ourselves from being destroyed. The care and help of a sick child often means that we are trying to bring through or reveal some secret value, but are having difficulty in helping this value to attain health in our compound constitution.

A dream of sickness often symbolizes self-pity. It is part of the same pattern that is expressed by the small boy who says to his mother, after having been punished, "When I'm dead, you'll be sorry." Many individuals who want to hurt other people's feelings have dreams that they are lying blissfully in a coffin, and all their enemies are weeping over them. This is a kind of revenge dream, a dream that has to do with getting even.

One of the most common psychological devices used by the person who wants to get even with circumstances, is symbolic self-destruction, which is most often expressed in dreams.

Dreams of battles usually indicate conflict within ourselves or with those around us. To be wounded in battle, therefore, is to feel psychic injury. To dream of being injured in an accident also tells of psychic injury that temporarily interferes with the individual's normal functioning. Symbols relating to various weapons are often quite interesting. Weapons generally represent the abilities of an adversary, powers or conditions of others for which we have no ready answer. A duel may symbolize a struggle of two attitudes or two levels of function; or it may indicate social struggle—a situation where the individual is out of harmony with his social stratum, or perhaps is trying to bluff and is therefore in danger of getting into difficulty. A fight or a very heated, unpleasant argument with other persons usually means stress and discord among the various departments of our own psychic life.

There are all kinds of adventure dreams, in which persons pass through various episodes similar to those in the mythologies of ancient peoples. In this type of dream, the individual involved usually becomes a kind of heroic person, and the dream becomes a hero dream. This is often similar to any one of the many legends from the age of fables. It may be paralleled in the Arabian Nights or in the wanderings of Odysseus; but wherever the person engages in a series of heroic exploits in his dreams, it is an indication that he is fighting psychologically against adversaries symbolized by the enemies in the dream.

There are certain types of dreams in which the symbolism reveals a more or less total psychological frustration. It is comparatively rare, however, for the dream to carry this frustration to the point of death. The individual may experience drowning, but he does not experience that he has drowned. He experiences falling, but he does not experience that the fall is actually fatal. He dreams that he is in trouble, that he is in a disaster, and it usually takes very little basic effort to clarify this situation in his thinking. He can begin to estimate the pressures around him, and he can relate to the general concept that he is being gradually absorbed into a situation over which he has no reasonable control. This dream of an impending vastness that he cannot hope to master, is almost always found to be a sign of extraordinary discouragement.

This type of dream may take any number of typical situations. A man may dream that he has been bitten by a serpent. It is several miles to the camp where he has snake anti-toxin. Every effort is made to prevent him from reaching that camp. He feels himself under the danger of death, he feels the poison spreading in him, he is striving desperately to get to this remedy; but obstacle after obstacle delays him. He may awaken in a cold sweat. He will probably not dream that the venom was fatal, but simply that he is struggling desperately against this danger.

In each person, the symbolism will be somewhat different, but dreams of the struggle to survive a hazard usually tell the elements of one story. Perhaps it is a dream of water rising and threatening to drown us; or darkness closing in, and we are like frightened children; or storms are breaking, and we have no shelter. All these types of dreams have to do with the individual's internal loss of hope. Psychologically, this is related to the letting go process in consciousness. The individual gives up his allotment of the love of life; it is being undermined. Something is happening around him that is causing him to fear the loss of his own life.

This loss of life idea is itself symbolical, because in the dream, life is not merely the continuity of the heartbeat. The meaning is extended to include not only physical continuance, but the continuance of the primary purposes of living. When we say a man wants to live his own life, what we really mean is that he will act as he pleases. It has nothing to do with physical continuity. Therefore, a man's life is his work, his dreams, his convictions, his hopes, his faith. It is almost anything by which he secures that vital impulse to continue to endeavor. So where the dream hazards life, it is actually hazarding the purposes of living. Dreams of this kind often arise where there are frustrations in personal affairs that seem to be hopeless, where the individual must either adjust without this sense of the loss of life, or give up. Therefore, the dream tells the individual that unless something is done to correct the situation, his ability to carry out his various functions in life will diminish.

The various symbols that suggest this are in one category basically, but there are certain differences in meanings. The individual who finds himself sinking in quicksand is having a somewhat parallel dream with the individual who finds himself drowning in the sea at night, but the difference between quicksand and the sea may or may not be important. It may mean simply the common sense of a loss of self-existence, but it may also suggest different types of danger. The quicksand problem nearly always implies that the person believes he is on firm ground, but is suddenly caught in an unexpected situation and finds himself slowly being destroyed. To drown suddenly in the ocean is a quicker kind of destruction, representing perhaps a more immediate crisis that must be immediately faced. But both the quicksand and the water, or whatever it may be, represent the individual's sense of losing contact with reality—the loss of a balanced, organized, suitable way of life. These things are subject to eternal improvisation, but the basic skeleton is relatively simple.

Religious dreams in general represent man reaching for security in time of stress. Therefore, both in waking and sleeping, emergency nearly always brings strong religious impact. The dream of being in church is generally either a symbol of internal integration or indicates the need for it. It may also signify the impulse to seek some form of solace. It is a recommendation to the consciousness of the individual to seek the solution to his problems through faith. Rituals of religion are usually indications of protection or of the availabiltiy of insight. Wherever religion appears constructively, it represents a contribution from the basic internal consciousness of the being. Where religion emerges in a dream as a persecuting or destroying force, it means a warning of the danger of prejudice arising in the person's psychic organization, which may turn upon him and injure him. Wherever a thing normally good takes on a malevolent aspect, we have misunderstood or misused a natural fact, and have therefore come under the displeasure, we might say, of that fact.

Dreams of celestial beings or divine persons generally represent one of two things: either that the individual is in an extremity, and is making a very strong plea to his basic faith, or that the individual is in the presence of a strong claim upon his life of some dedication or purpose. Frequently a person under very heavy responsibilities has a divine purpose dream, which assists him to carry his burdens because he comes to realize that he is fulfilling a spiritual need in his own life. And if the general pattern of this circumstance is benevolent, then this responsibility is proper. If the revelation takes on dogmatic or despotic attitudes, then his own willfulness is forcing him to stay with a situation that is otherwise not necessary or proper for him.

Thus, by means of the dream process, certain essential psychological verities may be revealed, so that the individual may receive a clearer insight into his own composition. In dreams, he receives the direct impact of pressures or disturbances that come to him in his physically conscious state only as obscure impulses with which he has to struggle throughout the day. The interpretation of dream symbols is made easier if the person immediately awakens and tries to relate his dreams to his own experiences just preceding sleep. In this way, many symbols otherwise difficult to understand can first be recognized and then more specifically analyzed. The first step is to determine the broad classification of the dream; the second, the definition of the major elements; and finally, the consideration of such details as may be comprehended. If this process is carried on carefully and thoughtfully, the individual will be able to interpret the majority of his dreams. Those more complicated may require the help of an analyst. For the most part, however, the individual can work these things out for himself. The dreams were meant for him; therefore, the power to use them is in him if he knows how to find that power.

PART V:
DREAMS OF WARNING OR PREMONITION

As we proceed to investigate forms of knowledge that have come down to us from the past, we become aware that our forefathers had a tendency to group together various types of phenomena without due consideration for the possibilities of varying causes. It was their general thinking that a broad area of similar effects could be attributed to a single cause, and as a result, we still have much to do in the search for the several answers that bear upon conditions apparently similar. We are trying to find reasons, and many things that appear the same, have different reasons behind them. This applies not only to physical health, but to a number of other situations.

Not so many years ago, for example, we considered the common cold and its various phases to be one ailment. Now we strongly suspect that there are many ailments involved. The symptoms are similar, but the causes are not identical. The same applies to the problem of dream phenomena. There can be more than one reason for a certain type of dream. There can be more than one explanation for what we now regard as a small group of related experiences. Therefore, when we come to consider the premonitional type of dream, or the dream that seems to bring a warning of some nature, and this dream proves to be prophetically accurate, we immediately try to pin down one explanation for the whole mystery. This, however, we cannot factually do. Therefore, under this general heading, we have to examine a number of possible causes for what apears to be a very single and definite occurrence.

One cause of premonitional and warning dreams arises in man's natural tendency to be fearful. There is a tendency in human nature to expect the unfortunate, particularly if we are depressed or suffering from some psychological pressure. This expectation passes through a number of different degrees, according to the temperament of the individual. It can also be based on the broad generalities of life. The individual whose life has been troubled, may broadly assume that his future will be troubled.

Nearly all premonitional dreams center upon disaster or trouble of some kind. We are not likely to prophesy something in the form of an unexpected good. Taking, for example, say a hundred dreams or strong intuitional pressures, we can come up with quite a variety of calamity warnings or forebodings. In the course of years, there have been a great many dreams relating to natural disasters. Almost every year, someone predicts a disastrous earthquake or flood. For the last fifty years, there has been a continuously maintained prophecy concerning the possible submergence of the entire Atlantic Seaboard of the United States. There is hardly a mail today that does not bring some worried question about whether a bomb will drop on Paducah or whether the Mississippi is going to overflow and become an ocean. This type of thinking is proverbial. For the last two thousand years, we have had regular end-of-the-world forebodings, which are often accompanied by dreams.

Up to the present time, probably ninety-five percent of these dreams of portending disaster are not fulfilled. Yet the individual, finding that the events do not occur, seems to lose no enthusiasm, and when he has failed in one prediction, he makes two more. Of course, in many instances, a prediction about a certain condition, if held long enough, may very well ultimately be fulfilled. For nearly twenty years, for example, a well-known English prophet annually announced the death of king George V. In the 20th year, he was right; and of course, under those conditions, the preceding nineteen years were merely minor errors in calculation. The principle remained untouched as far as this person was concerned, and he promptly went to work predicting the death of the next king. This type of situation seems to indicate man's natural tendency, under certain conditions, to fall into very negative attitudes.

We must also bear in mind that if we come under the influence of rather morbid statements, we may carefully nourish them and later release them as part of our own psychological pressure. We read something; we hear something; and because it is direful, it sort of clings to us if we have a slight tendency to the same attitude. In time, this subconsciously accepted statement comes out again as though it originated in ourselves, or perhaps in some larger circumstance. If it comes out as a remembrance of our original source of information, it makes no serious problem, but if it suddenly takes on the form of a vision or a dream sequence, it seems to be tremendously important. This type of thing was not uncommon in the medieval period, when many persons were dominated by a religious fixation relating to doom. They were convinced that the world might end at any moment, and as various millenial periods arose, these persons did have visions of the Last Judgment or the end of the world. This type of premonition arose very clearly from religious convictions, intensified by the corroboration of others with similar convictions, and even by the preachments of respected authorities.

Thus, if a fear mechanism is implanted in man, he has a tendency to enlarge upon it; to become continually expectant of some negative circumstance. This type of premonitional warning has really no essential validity. It is simply the individual interpreting circumstances from a negative point of view, or perhaps taking on some formula and working with it too desperately. We know, for example, that for a number of years, pyramid prophecies were attempted. These were based upon certain calculations that it was assumed had been incorporated into the structure of the Great Pyramid at Gizeh. In measuring these various areas and combinations of mathematical patterns, efforts were made to indicate major changes in human affairs. Wars, disasters, collapses of civilizations and cultures, were based upon nicks, scratches, small holes, and varying grains in the stones of the wall of the inner passageway of the pyramid. Obviously, you had to believe the basic premise in order to read the story as the author explained it or interpreted it; but many people became very fearful over some of these impending possibilities. This fearfulness, affecting the subconscious, caused visual occurrences in sleep that seemingly sustained this particular point of view.

Now, the juxtaposition of a premonition or a fear in relation to world events, means that in a certain percentage of cases, this type of dream would have a measure of fulfillment. If we expect certain things, and then interpret the intensities of world situations, something within ourselves, if it is only common sense, will indicate that many of our courses of action would reasonably lead to serious difficulties. We may therefore become fearful of things obvious and reasonable, and then dramatize this fearfulness in the form of some impending or presumed disaster. There is a certain degree of fulfillment always, because if we predict that man will be in trouble, we cannot be wrong very long. He has a decided tendency to do this, and it hardly requires a psychic perception to realize that many of our actions can only end in trouble. Thus, perhaps we are secretly telling ourselves the kind of consequences that are inherent in our own actions.

This type of explanation does not cover the entire ground by any means; but it does, perhaps, cover a certain superficial group of conditions that are present and are undoubtedly responsible for the fact that so many of these predictions fail utterly to materialize.

Another situation that we cannot deny, nor adequately explain for that matter, is that many important events go unpredicted. I know individuals, for example, who spent practically every hour of their sleeping time dramatizing impending disasters, and yet missed entirely a very serious one that occurred in the course of their period of dramatization. The same thing happens in so-called psychic situations. One person I knew really believed that he was psychically in tune with just about everything. He announced wars and pestilences and plagues and practically every type of disaster; but he was sitting in Long Beach when the earthquake occurred there, and he had not the slightest idea it was coming. Thus, many things predicted do not occur, and many things that no one anticipates actually happen. For this reason, I think we must be very careful in estimating this type of mental phenomenon.

One of the reasons, perhaps, why the individual is somewhat inclined to feel that evil is ever nigh unto him, is because down inside the deepest parts of his own conscience, he has decided that he is honestly entitled to trouble. He knows that he has so conducted his own affairs that they are not in order, not secure, and are therefore subject to innumerable shocks. Consciously, he may defend against this, but subconsciously, the truth will out. Persons who have planned badly, invested poorly, been imposed upon too easily, inwardly realize that this type of circumstance must cause trouble ultimately. Consequently, they may warn themselves. They cannot warn themselves consciously, because many persons are unwilling to admit in their conscious moods that they make mistakes. But the subconscious part of them, which is a little more honest and a better record keeper, will very often warn them of impending inevitables.

Since dream symbolism is seldom literal, the dream that accompanies this type of warning will present one kind of a disaster to reveal or imply another. A person whose investments are going badly, may dream that he is drowning in a very stormy sea. What nature is trying to tell him is that he is insecure; that the things he is doing are not according to his own common sense; that he has come under the glamor of the hope of high reward for small effort. This is more than his conscious mind can handle, but inside each of us is a realist who can and does face facts. This realist may whisper in our ears that trouble is approaching, but in order to reach us, it has to break through our objective attitudes; and this is best accomplished when we are asleep.

This overcoming of conscious resistance is well illustrated in the following case history of a woman who had a dream that worried her gravely. She had two sons—fine, up-and-coming young men, and one night she dreamed that these two sons were coming home, returning to the family for some holiday, and along the way they passed through a serious storm. In this storm, the ground turned into quicksand, and these two boys sank and died. Naturally, the mother wondered whether this was a true warning that these boys' lives were in danger. In the course of some months, no factual incident to corroborate the dream occurred—in fact, none ever occurred; and that was a number of years ago. But something was happening. This mother was an extremely possessive person, well intentioned in every way, but instinctively holding on too firmly upon the lives of these two young men. Apparently, this symbolism of coming back to the family for the celebration was a fulfillment of the mother's desire to prevent the boys from going out into the world and living their own lives. She wanted them to come back; she wanted to continually protect them. But symbolically, something in her was telling her that if these boys came back, returned again to her influence there would be a storm, a struggle for their own independence, and that finally their individuality would be destroyed and they would sink into the quicksand of her emotional possessiveness and domination.

This was being told to her by her own inner insight. Yet in her conscious mind, she was so desirous of continuing to have the pleasure of directing these young men, that she did not for a moment suspect that anything she could wish for them or do for them could hurt them in any way. Later when a conflict did arise, and one of the young men wished to get married, the mother developed an intense hysteria over the whole thing. Then the dream became meaningful, and when it was interpreted, the real facts began to reveal themselves. Fortunately, the mother was able to accept the meaning, which she knew inside was true, and to take hold of herself and prevent the psychological drowning of her sons. The dream, therefore, did warn of something—it was a premonition, but it was not a literal or factual premonition.

This is a very important guide, because it serves two purposes. First, it shows that the dream does have a meaning; second, it indicates the error of literalizing the symbolism and then feeling that there was no meaning because the physical events do not occur. Just as the mass ill fortune dream usually only signifies the negativeness in ourselves, so particular dreams often indicate our tendencies or habits that are leading us into trouble.

If, then, we have dreams relating to some emergency to those around us, we should do very well to examine our relationships with these other persons, to discover what kind of an adroit scheme we are holding in relation to those persons. Usually there is a little scheme of some kind— something that to us is perfectly reasonable and normal, which we do not sense as dishonest, but which perhaps is ethically not really honest. It is much the same type of thing as intense competitiveness in business. We justify competition because apparently everyone practices it, and without it we are unable to survive. In the name of competition, we do things that are not ethically correct, although we may break no physical law, nor subject ourselves to any legal action. We are just not quite honest. And in personal relationships, this is a very common circumstance. We do not honestly estimate what we deeply love or what we hate. Wherever the emotions and attitudes of the individual become intensely involved, common sense, factual thinking, realization, and reality depart. The only way we can perhaps save ourselves from the consequences is to listen to the internal value that lies locked in our own souls.

Another type of warning dream is called the *prodromic dream.* This is a symptomological dream, in which the individual dreams in a diagnostic way about his own health. Somehow the internal chemistry of man, particularly when it has been attacked by the inroads of disease, affects the entire psychic life, and sickness may be felt subconsciously before it is consciously recognized. One of the reasons for this may well be that disturbance of the psyche may be the cause of the sickness. This increasing hazard to the total integration of the person creates mental-emotional stress patterns of a peculiar nature, which can become intuitively known. The physical system, even though it is extremely sensitive, is not as sensitive as the psychic organism, and by the time certain symptoms have worked their way out into our physical objective awareness, a great deal of symptomology has already occurred that was cognized only by the subconscious part of ourselves.

This may have been one of the explanations of the old clinics of Aesculapius, the Greek god of healing. These clinics strongly emphasized dream diagnosis. The patient was brought into the temple, given a sleep-inducing herb of some kind, and then in his sleep, the deity seemed to appear to him and diagnose the ailment, and sometimes the therapy indicated. Primarily, this was undoubtedly the unlocking of man's own interior power to know the condition of himself. When this breaks through in dreams, it may very well do so symbolically. The event may not be exactly what the dream seems to mean, but there is a valid relationship that can be interpreted. A classsic example of this is the story of the man who dreamed that he was swimming in an ocean of blood, and a few days later had a hemorrhage. This particular dream certainly was a diagnostic one. The psyche knew what was coming, because the causes of the circumstance were already at work within the body, although the person was not aware of them. One of the reasons the psyche might have had this awareness is that it was able to judge the nature of the person and his actions, his previous conduct in certain matters—perhaps habits or practices that weaken the body, or some previous exertion that endangered the body and made this hemorrhage especially likely.

Nature has a tendency to warn things. It does not wish them to fall into disaster. In fact, a large part of the sensory structure of man is defensive, intended to assist him in the protection of his life. It is his own tendency to ignore the help provided by nature that causes him to have more and more trouble. Nature, trying to break through with one of its helpful warnings, usually chooses the sleep period, because then the self-will of the individual is subordinated. These experiences of a clear statement of truth come when the defense mechanisms of opinion and attitude have been temporarily suspended. Since sleep really represents the temporary relief from psychic stress, we can extend this thinking to the realization that if the individual can consciously relieve himself of this stress, can relax and become quietly receptive to basic ideas, he will usually be able to discover what he needs to know. It is the tension under which we operate that actually permits us to make mistakes. If we were relaxed and thoughtful, if we were conscientious in tracing through the patterns of our own conduct, we would be able to save ourselves innumerable tragic hours. We have the power, but it only operates when we get out of the way of our own self-interest—a false self-interest that is hurting us instead of helping, because it seeks merely to fulfill our desires, not to support our needs.

There is another possible level of explanation for the diagnostic type of dream phenomenon. We know that certain persons, especially if they are trained, recognize ailments more quickly than others. Now, we are speaking of ailment not necessarily as a physical condition, but as anything that has a tendency to disturb or endanger the order or normalcy of existence. We know that it is perfectly possible to detect from the general structure of the person, from his reactions to certain situations, how he is likely to fare in this world. If he does not pass certain tests, he will have troubles throughout life. The troubles are not the result of failing the test, but of a condition within himself, of which the test failure is merely a demonstration.

Thus, the entire psychic integration of the individual gives a very clear picture of what is most likely to happen to him. And because the details of his character help to define the details of events likely to occur, we can come very close to a remarkably accurate prophecy about someone merely as the result of the daily exhibition he makes of the attributes of his disposition. We know that certain attitudes will have certain consequences. We may not be able to date the consequences, but we are fully aware that they will occur; and sometimes they come more rapidly than we realize. The more pronounced the symptom, the more rapidly the consequence will be manifested.

The lesson that this tries to teach us is that we should search for these indications ourselves; that we should become as mindful as we can of processes that can cause trouble, correcting them ourselves, and placing a long-range strategy in our minds. We so frequently forget that time passes rapidly. If an individual at twenty is told that a certain course of action will make him ill at forty, he is very likely to say, "Remind me at thirty-nine, and I'll do something about it." We do not like to give immediate thought to remote happenings. But these twenty years go by with unbelievable rapidity, and suddenly, that impending event has come to its fruition, and we are faced with it. By that time, it may have progressed to a degree where we can do very little about it. This putting off of necessary changes in ourselves is a very false way to seek happiness or comfort, because the purposes of nature will undoubtedly assert themselves with almost mathematical finality.

The psychosomatic relationship between certain policies and health, or the relationship between character and the probability of successful marriage, or between inner maturity and our ability to direct the lives of our children—these things are certain and factual; but we are not always willing to face them. Yet subconsciously they build up toward their inevitable conclusions. Most psychic stress is due to this conflict between the surface purposes of the individual and the subconscious facts that are constantly trying to impress him, trying to come through into consciousness in order that he may take advantage of the truths they reveal.

Let us assume for a moment that an individual is living a rather badly integrated life, which is gradually destroying the relationship between his body and his psycho-nervous system. He is worrying too much; he is frightened over some situation that has arisen; he has lacked courage; he is drifting; he is postponing necessary decisions; he is confused; he is gradually going down for the third time in a sea of his own troubles. This situation, going on and on over a period of time, will ultimately result in what might be termed psychic exhaustion. He will come in the end to what we know as a nervous breakdown. Or he will continue policies and practices until he destroys perhaps his business, or his home, or his social standing. Inside himself, his own psychic life is telling him that something is wrong, but he is not quite able to bring these patterns together; he still remains without a sense of the answer that is necessary to meet this emergency.

Finally, in the course of this process of gradual suicide, he comes to one of these early morning hour periods in which his own psychic life that knows better—his overself, as Emerson called it—comes through to him in a dream. It may come in the form of a warning of the impending difficulty, or it may be a diagnosis, or it may take the form of simply revealing to him the direction of his own troubles. He may awaken with an allegorical concept rather strongly in his mind, such as the story of the two men—one who built his house on a rock, and the other, on sand. Perhaps he will dream that he is standing on sand that gives way beneath him; or that he is caught in some morass or swamp. Perhaps he will dream that some strange disaster hangs over his head. Thus, the subconscious draws upon stories and legends that we know, in the effort to clothe basic impulses that are themselves usually formless. Such dreams can constitute a warning, and cause the individual to seek psychological help, especially if the dream is repeated. Or it may be that the dream is enough to cause him to make a conscious effort to direct his own courses more wisely.

In some cases, the dream may come as a direct therapy in itself. For example, he may learn by subconscious knowledge that he is in a career that is not proper for him. There are cases where persons in the wrong occupation have actually had the dream that either they were on the wrong road, or they had come down a street on their way home and had gotten into the wrong house. This "wrong house" symbolism is very interesting, because it means, essentially, a wrong way of life—a wrong habitation for the character. One man had a dream that he went into a house which he thought was his own, and it proved to be somebody else's house, and then he saw himself dead in the front room. This dream, therefore, is telling the individual that his way of life is wrong, and that if he continues in this way, he will not survive. Now, whether he is physically dead, or whether it symbolizes the fact that as long as he is in this wrong house he will be as though dead, is not the main issue. The point is that in his present situation, which is wrong, nothing will ever truly come to life for him.

Perhaps this man then rushes out of the house in his dream experience, and runs down the street. He is terrified, he is half sick, he does not know what is going to happen, and he looks in various directions to find where he should go. Finally, he comes to a church, and he rushes into the church and falls down on his knees to pray. Now, this is not really telling him to go to church—these psychic experiences are not that literal. It is telling him that he needs the consolation of understanding; that he is deficient in faith, and has not sought inner guidance. The church is almost always a symbol of divine or inner guidance. And the recommendation is, of course, that he listen more to the inside, and less to the outside; that he depend less upon his own objective mind, and more upon this intuitive power that men have always symbolized as a divine principle in themselves.

Dreams of this kind seem to imply, in many instances, the element of foreknowledge. A person who dreams of an accident or injury, for example, may be quite upset by this dream, assuming that it is a literal thing. More than likely, however, the dream represents a symbolic accident, and is trying to tell the person that if he continues in a certain course of procedure, something will happen. One man dreamed that he was trying to run away from something that seemed very difficult, and as he ran out into a road, he was struck by a car. He had the sense of being struck, but as is usual in dreams, he did not have the actual experience of dying. The psychic shock of being struck by the car awakened him. Six months later, his home fell apart, and he found himself with a divorce on his hands. He had been trying to run away from certain characteristics. In so doing, he had undermined the stability of his home; and finally, the breaking of the home was represented by the accident, which struck him down. In this case, the problem was the individual's evasion of maturity.

He refused psychologically to accept the responsibility of being a husband and a parent. Consciously, he would not acknowledge this, and when the home finally broke, he was completely astonished. But actually, his subconscious knew all the time that his way of procedure could produce no other consequence. The dream indicated that he was in a panic—that he was trying to run away from the situation. Subconsciously, he knew what was coming.

So these dreams can take generally prophetic forms, because as soon as the incident occurs, we are able to say that this is obviously what the dream meant. But until something does happen, we are rather careful for fear that it might be a literal accident that is implied. In some cases, a physical accident may be indicated, and it may actually occur, but in the majority of instances, it is a symbolic one.

The average person who comes under dream analysis, or who deals with this phase of his own inner life, is not essentially a prophet; nor is he basically a mystic. He is usually a person of comparatively imperfect attainment who is in need of immediate help in the most simple and commonplace occurrences. The individual who thinks he is far beyond the problems of ordinary mortals suddenly finds himself confronted with a broken home, or sees his business evaporating through poor management. It has not occurred to him that such things could happen to him. He believes that he has gone far beyond this in his internal insight; but he has falsely weighed his own attainment. I think it is wise to assume, therefore, that the average person does not have available extrasensory faculties which may normally be the explanation of unusual occurrences. What he calls extrasensory faculties are really his own true faculties, which he has not been willing to acknowledge, or which he has misinterpreted. And the voice that comes is not the voice of an angel, but the voice of his own desperately afflicted nature trying to correct him. It is trying to bring him in line with realities, to help him find himself in the midst of erroneous conclusions about himself, which, if continued, would merely get him further and further into trouble.

We must also bear in mind, however, that there are certain evidences of premonitional or warning experiences which do not conveniently fit into these suggested causations. One of the most difficult of these to analyze is the so-called "dated" dream, or the vision in which an occurrence is clearly located in its time sequence. This kind of dream may not be essentially personal—in fact, it very often is not personal. For example, there was a case of a small boy who had a very clear and vivid dream of the great earthquake disaster of Martinique years ago. This child sat up in the night screaming, and described the occurrence. A day or two later, Martinique was struck exactly as this boy had seen. Now, he had no interest in Martinique—he probably did not know it existed. He had no reason to suddenly become so highly sensitive and to prevision even the details of this disaster.

The psychological explanation that we have previously advanced for premonitional dreams obviously is simply not adequate for this type of dream occurrence. On the other hand, the explanation for this type of prognostic dream should not merely be enlarged to make it cover all the others. The fact that this boy undoubtedly had an authentic example of a premonitional dream, does not mean that all other dreams of disaster warnings are authentically premonitional; nor that the faculties used by this boy are the same faculties used by the individual in a dream of another disaster which does not occur. We must therefore try to analyze the genuine prophetic dream, which cannot be explained, as far as we can determine, by psychic disturbance within the person.

This type of prophetic dream usually has a different dimension in its presentation, in that it is not symbolical, but literal. It describes the event exactly as it is, instead of fighting its way through the symbol-making mechanism of our consciousness. From the general study of this kind of dream phenomenon, there is much to indicate that it represents a direct impact from some source outside of the psychic mechanism of the individual. This, of course, leads immediately to the consideration of such things as telepathy, extrasensory perception, and the possibility of true and valid foreknowledge about events that are to occur.

The foreknowledge type of dream suggests that there may be some condition in nature by means of which larger impending patterns have an existence before the occurrences to which they are related. Thus, we must assume that the Martinique earthquake, or other earthquakes of a similar nature, have some kind of laws governing them, and that an individual can become aware of the procedure that is leading to the disaster. In other words, the earthquake must exist before it happens.

This seems to be utterly impossible, and yet accurate prophecy is considered equally impossible. One school has thought it out in this rather intriguing way—namely, that disasters represent the outworkings of natural law; that a disaster has to be much like a sickness in the body, the result of adequate cause long operating. The timing of a disaster, or the timing of a sickness in the body, however, may be due to the great clock in the sky—that is, the massing of planetary power. The planets do not cause the disaster, but they precipitate it. For example, a person under a certain type of stress may have a long-enduring tendency to a thrombosis. This thrombosis could come at any time, once it is established as a probability. Yet the actual occurrence may often be determined from a horoscope, because the planetary relationships indicate periods of stress or strain that will precipitate into fact the long-existing tendency.

Now, it is conceivable that man can be sufficiently sensitive to these psychic influences, or to these groupings of planetary force, that he can become aware within himself of the pattern that is going to affect something else. In other words, he can sense or experience without mentation the qualities of the pressure or massing of planetary rays. Thus, he becomes a subconscious or unconscious estimator of the intensities of the vibrations in the atmosphere around him; and as these vibrations, in turn, are localized on principles of geodetic equivalents, he may even be aware of the area in which these vibrations will center. Just as he can train himself outwardly to read, with some degree of accuracy, the relation of the stars to a nativity, so perhaps he can read them even better subconsciously, without even knowing what he is doing. He simply receives the pure impact of the archetypal energy itself, and then proceeds to differentiate this energy in himself, discovering in the process the meaning of the energy.

This might seem like a rather circuitous way of doing things, but there is no doubt in the world that human beings can know intuitively. There is also no doubt that most so-called forms of fortune telling—whether they be according to the *I Ching* of the Chinese, or according to the geomancy practiced by the old Roman soldiers, or according to mechanical devices such as cards or dice—are interpretations. And the interpretations arise not in the symbols themselves, but in the person who interprets them. In the same way, one physician may be extremely intuitive in his diagnosis, so that there is really little need for him to make use of laboratory facilities at all. He senses the type of problem the sick person is suffering from. Other physicians do not possess this sensitivity, and must depend upon laboratory reports. The tendency in medicine, however, is that the practitioner who is sympathetic, understanding, and is largely dominated by the true principles of healing will, through the course of years, intensify his own sensitivity. He gradually develops an interior power to estimate what is to occur on what is wrong.

It is quite conceivable, by the same procedure, that the highly sensitive person, who is always responsive to the psychic forces around him, will be able to find in nature certain patterns that can be diagnosed. Nature cannot be merely blind forces moving blindly. If such were the case, no predictions could be made. There has to be a pattern, a scientific unfoldment of archetypes, which the sufficiently sensitive person can understand by intuition.

We assume that man's physical body is a sort of mirror which reflects his psychic life, so that his physical personality becomes the extension of a series of causal factors behind it. Let us assume for a moment that the physical earth is such a body; that this earth is really the visible part of an elaborate structure, and that the invisible parts of this structure correspond to the emotional, mental, and psychic life of man. The predispositions to various physical conditions would then lie within the invisible parts of the structure, and what we call a physical circumstance would arise from invisible factors. These factors group, and when a group becomes sufficiently dominant, then the earthbody will receive an impression and be modified and molded accordingly.

According to this thinking, things happening in the visible nature have an antecedent existence. They do not simply happen, but are motions of values moving into a precipitant state. They are gradually intensifying until they become factual or dominant in the material world. Let us use a parallel in human affairs. An individual starts out with a pretty decent disposition, and then he begins to develop a habit that caters to some negative factor in his personality. At first he nags a little; well, anyone can nag a little—most people do. But in this particular individual, the occasional nagging produces immediate results that seem to fascinate him. He nags a little; he gets what he wants. Other people say, "Oh well, let's do it his way if that's what he wants." So he wins. Now, having won by a negative action that was not especially meritorious, and having a natural tendency to be habit-ridden, this person really develops into a first-class nagger. At first he nags once a month, then once a week, then once a day, and finally all the time. Finally, it is no longer an expedient nagging, but someting that he can no longer control. It becomes like a habit addiction, a tremendous pressure, and all his will power cannot get him over this instinctive habit. It may destroy many values for him, but he cannot stop.

Now, this pattern builds up for a long time, and perhaps for a considerable period, the nagging produces no visible result, except to get this person what he wants. But after many years of this problem, the crisis comes. The family gets tired of it, and some very small nagging incident, occurring at a critical moment, causes the family to leave him. The action finally occurred one afternoon; but the cause of it had been building up for twenty years, and the moment came that precipitated the inevitable effect. Now, at the beginning of the twenty years, perhaps no one could have foreseen where this nagging was going to lead. But six months before the break came, any good analyst could have described very clearly what was going to happen, because the reactions of all the persons had become so conditioned that it was merely a matter of time before the family would disintegrate. Tuning in at one of these later points by subconscious means, any individual who was intuitive could have announced the broken home. He probably could not have predicted the day on which it would occur, but he could have said that the condition would not extend much longer—that it was only a matter of months, or a year or two. These things represent patterns building up.

World patterns also build up. The psycho-historian can see them. He realizes that competition, extravagance, the continuance of unsolved problems among nations, the gradual results of the industrial changes forced upon people—ultimately, these things are going to come to a head. Something is going to break; major changes will occur. If we estimate these patterns objectively by reason, we call our discovery of what will happen "judgment," but if our conscious judgment is not up to it, and this pattern strikes against our subconscious psychic integration, it is still judgment, but it appears to us as a flash of intuition. It appears as miraculous foreknowledge. But the miraculous element is simply due to the fact that we have not recognized that all processes in nature are natural. The miracle is merely a process that we do not understand, but which must also be natural.

There is no question that in the world's psychological atmosphere, as in man's personal psycho-emotional atmosphere, vast motions of world affairs are in various degrees of precipitation. There is no doubt that through a proper receptivity to the degree of development of these psychic patterns, we may predict with reasonable certainty the probability of the timing of a war. We can predict national declines and things of that nature, if our subjective faculties are able to estimate the processes that are taking place around us in life.

There have been recorded cases where an individual dreamed about an accident or some event in the future that would actually involve him personally. For example, a man dreamed that the train on which he rode to the city every day was going to be wrecked. He saw the incident clearly, even to the day on which the accident would occur; and he saw himself apparently in this wreck. When the day came, he simply refused to get on the train. He warned his friends, but most of them paid no attention to him, thinking it was merely some kind of hysteria. The train was wrecked, but he was not on it.

These things are very difficult to explain. The first thing we know is that the person did not consciously have this record. The train had made this run for probably twenty years without a previous accident. It was not something that would be normally likely to be in his subconscious. Actually, therefore, there is only one answer—namely, that the subconscious or the superconscious, or whatever lies behind the objective consciousness, has the power of a certain kind of foreknowledge, and that this foreknowledge may be available to certain persons at certain times. Why it is not available to other persons is a question that perhaps goes back to the Eastern ideas of karmic compensation. In any event, some persons apparently either have so altered their destinies by their own conduct that they are entitled to escape from these emergencies; or for some reason, they were not intended to be involved, and had to be protected.

There is a belief in the Orient that is perhaps as good an answer as any until we find a better one—and it is going to take quite a little finding. This Eastern belief is that the entity comes into birth with a certain karmic debt, and this karmic responsibility is usually very much larger than could possibly be compensated for in a single lifetime. Now, at a certain period in the process of embodiment, the entity, as a psychic being, is shown the record. It is shown the debt it has to pay, and how that debt will be paid—that is, the various circumstances involved. Therefore, as far as the psychic entity is concerned, there can never be a moment when the psychic being does not understand what is happening to it. In other words, there can never be any doubt, in the higher part of man's nature, concerning the honesty of the situations in which he is involved, but the objective consciousness is not aware of this. Therefore, it is possible that the archetypal image of the total course of a life and the debts and lessons peculiar to that embodiment in terms of its karma, may be available to the psychic entity. This availability then becomes the basis of an immediate prophetic power. Thus, there has to be an archetypal motion behind everything that occurs. Every event that we see has to be a seed breaking through ground into visibility, its invisible part lying in its karmic relationship to life and in the causes that produce it.

If there is an archetypal, or akashic, record—not only of things that have happened, but of the natural unfoldment of the life collective according to its own destiny—then the relationship of man to the common destiny may be available to the consciousness of the individual. In any event, incidents of this kind have occurred, and no simple explanation that will be acceptable by all, scientific and otherwise, is likely to be found. The only answer has to be that there are dimensions of archetypal records in nature that are beyond our explanation, and that in these archetypal records there is a certain area in which the future is almost fatalistically conditioned by present circumstances. And this relative future can be grasped or known psychically.

Thus, the person's place in this relative future can be anticipated. Where the anticipation does not occur, where the individual goes quietly to his destiny without ever knowing that it is his destiny—obviously, under those conditions, the pattern works in its complete operation. But suppose for a moment, that man, being an individual, has made certain basic changes in his own temperament along the course of his lifetime. These changes may alter or condition his destiny, for with man as a self-conscious being, destiny cannot be fatalistic. Thus if the individual changes, it is possible that the psychic life within him is given the problem, or the responsibility, of adjusting his relationship to events to meet the psychological changes in his nature. Therefore, one person may be warned, and ten are not. Ten persons may pass through the same experience, and one survives.

I believe that the dream that deals with events to come merely represents the fact that the psychic nature is aware of these things. But if this awareness were made available generally to the objective life, the entire process of destiny would be frustrated. If the individual were in a position to foreknow his own destiny and avert it, without merit or reason, he would no longer be operating with nature. The only way a person can justly avoid a destiny is to outgrow it; and if he does not outgrow it, then he has no right to change it.

Certain dreams of a premonitional or warning nature can be explained by telepathy or extrasensory perception. Take for instance a case where a person dreams that his father is dying, and then receives a telegram the next morning saying that the father has passed on. This type of dream is almost certainly due to a psychical sympathy. Many explanations have been given for this phenomenon, but there are two that seem to me most valid. The first is the psychic sympathy of blood. This mysterious thing we call blood is highly individual. It descends in families, and the members of a family therefore have a psychic rapport through the magnetic field of the blood. This is borne out by the strange rapport that exists between identical twins. The second answer is that the psychic field of the individual is also a kind of blood, and that the psychic fields of persons related by blood or by great attachment of another kind, are attuned to each other so as to make it possible for these persons to be aware of what occurs to each other. This is essentially the Paracelsian concept of sympathetic energies.

Now, we may point out, against this theory, that many persons having such apparent sympathy are still not aware of these occurrences. Three children are involved when a parent dies—two of them are not at all aware of it, but the third has a premonitional dream. The answer here seems to lie in the sensitivity of the one individual, and his ability to project impulse into a dream phenomenon. Perhaps there was also a stronger internal psychic attachment than the others possessed, or some special relationship to the parents by which the one individual was caused to have the impression. But where a thing of this nature occurs, it is almost certainly a matter of telepathy. Any dream that depends upon some form of knowledge about what someone else is doing, and which can be explained by a transference of thought, is probably best considered on that level until we go further. This explanation should not, however, be held as dogmatic, for it is possible that in this so-called telepathic area of dreams, there may be a dozen subdivisions, with various factors involved in the transmission of the dream impulse.

Clairvoyance in dreams is different from thought transference or the generally accepted concept of extrasensory perception, in that it may involve occurrences happening at a distance, in which the individual has no known psychic relationship. The person, for example, may dream that he is traveling in another land, and may become aware of things happening in that land, or may see events that do not have any particular bearing on him personally. If these events are actually occurring at the time of the dream, or follow the dream closely, then it is quite probable that it is a genuine case of clairvoyance. If, however, the event does not coincide with the dream, but still happens ultimately, then pure clairvoyance, or the ability to see or to know a thing at a distance, will not answer the question.

Many of the American Indian medicine priests had the power, according to the testimony and experiences of their people, of being able to locate herds of animals at a distance. The old priest would simply sit down and quietly meditate, and send his consciousness up and down the wilderness to find the herds. This, however, is not the same as prophecy. What he has actually done, according to his own teaching, is that he has been to the place and has seen the herd there. He has been able to project his consciousness, and this projection was consciously recorded not as a journey to the herd, but as a visualization, in a dream, of its location. Most of the wisdom and instructions of the old priests were recorded in the dream sequence form, because the inward experience broke through to their outer consciousness in this way.

We can say, therefore, that dreams which indicate the general direction of events can be the result of a number of different factors. There is clairvoyance, telepathy, and the possibility of extraordinary development of acute judgment on a psychic level. Some of these dreams may be due to the pressure of our own internal and inevitable self-demands; some may be the stamping of the psychic nature's own directives upon our lives; some represent the true meaning of ourselves coming through to us. All these various aspects can arise from the different levels of our own consciousness, and can involve faculties and perceptions beyond our present general acceptance. The dream phenomenon is not as simple as many people believe it to be; there is much more to be learned.

PART VI:
THE DREAM AS VISION
OR MYSTICAL EXPERIENCE

Knowledge has come to man through the dream-vision experience since the very beginning of his existence. Even today among primitive groups, the final emergencies of life are met by the dream. When the individual is unable to secure any practical insight from ordinary means, he goes into meditation or prayer, departs from the world, or seeks the assistance of some mystic, and then, in mystical trances and dreams and visions, he finds the concrete answers to problems that he cannot otherwise solve.

Visions are unquestionably types of psychical experiences derived principally from within ourselves. For the most part, a vision is a valid kind of dream. It is a dream of meaning, of purpose. It is a dream of communication between the inner and the outer life of the individual, which projects upon the individual some larger value, perhaps of a highly spiritual nature, that could not be impressed upon him by reason or argument. The dream as vision or mystical experience has a peculiar validity because it is so totally our own. It makes something that would otherwise be impossible or incredible both acceptable and useful.

The great example of such an experience is the Theophany of St. Paul. It would have been comparatively impossible to have argued Paul into a state of Christian acceptance. It is doubtful if any scholar could have achieved it, or if any amount of reading or study would have converted him, because he was convinced that the religion he was following had the sanction of his God. Yet somewhere in his early contact with Christianity, something must have moved Paul profoundly. That which he could not accept consciously must have awakened some form of subconscious realization in his own nature. The mystical experience of Paul therefore came as a tremendous internal release. It was the power of something locked in him over the power of his own conscious believing— his inner life bursting through.

In order to understand the psychological significance of the Theophany of Paul, we must recall some of the circumstances surrounding the occurrence. It is described, in the older apocryphal writings at least, that he was riding to Damascus to persecute the Christian community there. He had already attacked one of the disciples and injured him in physical combat, and Paul was very close to a situation in which a great war of values was being fought within his own psychic nature. Not being a persecuting man by nature, it must have been difficult for him to feel that his religion required him to persecute someone else. It might well be, therefore, that as he was on his way to the final act of persecution, the conflict within him became unendurable, so that a tremendous psychic revulsion set in. This revulsion may have then taken the form of the simple question that came to him in the vision—a question that he probably asked himself: why did he persecute these people? This question came through in all its force, and from that time on, Paul persecuted no more.

The vision itself is described as having occurred in a flash of light—a great burst of radiance. Paul fell from his horse, stunned, and lay on the ground, temporarily blinded. In the midst of this tremendous psychic stress, Paul experienced the theophany. In one account, it is implied that he actually saw Jesus, and that Jesus spoke to him. In another account, in the same Bible, Paul did not claim to have seen any person—only a great light, and a voice spoke to him out of the light; and this voice undoubtedly spoke the very words that Paul's own soul was crying out to utter.

There are several possible explanations for the pressure of this experience. Some have suggested that because of the nature of the region and the conditions, a sunstroke or heat prostration might well have been a contributing cause. Others have gone so far as to say that the experience represented a convulsion, or some kind of an epileptic seizure. In any event, it carried a tremendous psychic impact. Paul was still blind, it is said, when he reached Damascus, and his sight was restored to him by one of the Elders of the Christian community there.

Here we have a very interesting and almost complete problem for modern psychoanalysis. It would seem that this was not an experience in which an evil man was suddenly transformed into a good man by an act of providence. This act of providence was Paul himself, as indicated by his ministry from that time on. Such a ministry could have arisen only in a man with great courage of character, great dedication to principles, and a profound respect for truth in all of its aspects.

Thus we see that a vision can be, and probably often is, the statement of a reality inwardly held, but not outwardly accepted. Man may well be better inside than he is on the outside. He may well know more, because as we go into the inner part of man, we also come to the superior aspects of his consciousness. Whatever is the best of man is locked at the core of his being. And as he reaches further toward that core, he becomes aware of greater value, and is therefore more impelled to commendable actions.

Many visions of the general type of the Theophany of Paul have been reported, and the canonizations of a great many of the early saints of the Church are based on such visions. And these experiences still occur, not only among Christians, but among nearly all peoples. These visions nearly always bestow the strength for a voluntary allegiance to a greater and better cause, or to a fuller expression of some great spiritual reality.

The vision may occur in a condition or time not normally associated with sleep. In the case of St. Paul, we find that the actual occurrence was preceded by a shock or some mysterious force that cast him into a state of confusion and comparative unconsciousness. The light that burst upon his consciousness and hurled him to the ground was a kind of power that paralyzed him completely, and made it impossible for him to maintain any objective mental integration. And it was in the midst of this suspension of all his worldliness that the significant part of the vision was transmitted.

We do not assume, of course, that everyone has so vital or startling an example of this peculiar psychic process, but we do know that nearly everyone has an availability—a means of reaching into self—if an emergency should demand it. There are innumerable cases of visions of varying degrees that have led to powerful changes in the lives of the individual who experienced them. The vision is not unknown to scientists, although, because of their strong intellectual orientation, it is not as common with them as it is with persons of a more simple and devout mentality. Simplicity is a point with which nature seems to be profoundly concerned. Most mystics, particularly those of Asia and of early Christianity, instinctively cultivated a kind of simplicity of life and thought. They were seldom to be considered as sophisticated persons. Many of them were not scholars as we understand scholarship. They were pious persons, living in an almost continual state of prayer or of strong and abiding faith. As a result, they were almost always psychically relaxed. Under such conditions, the availability of the mystical experience is greater than it is for ordinary persons.

Plotinus, the great Neoplatonist, describes two or three visions that occurred to him during his lifetime. Plotinus was a philosopher, a man of powerful mind and most penetrating genius. He was one of the outstanding intellectual leaders of his time. Yet he was not a sophisticate or a worldly man. He was not a seeker after knowledge for the sake of knowledge. He was primarily a mystic, and Neoplatonism, which derived so much from him, is considered today as a mystical rather than an essentially philosophical doctrine.

The mystical experiences described by Plotinus lasted only a brief time, were very rare of happening, but profoundly affected his life. In those moments, it seemed that he was lifted up and brought into identity with reality. He had a peculiar sense of belongingness. He was one with space, with life, and with eternity. He found his true relationship to existence—a relationship of profound sympathy, which brought both tears and laughter to his soul. In this relationship, the universality of the Good became not realized or believed, but perfectly and fully known by a total conscious experience of fact. These experiences of Plotinus certainly must be included among the great historical mystical occurrences.

We know, also, that most of the Book of John, known as the Apocalypse, or the Revelation of John on the Island of Patmos, was written as a dream, or as a mystical experience. John did not know whether he was in the flesh or not; he was simply separated from worldliness, and in this separation, the vision of the Apocalypse was unfolded to him. Here, again, is a mystical revelation arising from previous personal experiences, from previous knowledge and indoctrination received from the religious community in which he dwelt for a time on the Island of Patmos. He was close to some of the greatest centers of ancient pre-Christian mysticism. We have here many factors, perhaps revealing much of the background of John that would not be recorded by the Gospel historians. It is the story of the inner life of the man, which finally blazed out in the vision of the Apocalypse.

Thus, these visions do have some valid relationship to our own peculiar problems and needs. The visions always end with a kind of clarification. The problem becomes ensouled by a power greater than itself, and by this very process, ceases to be a problem. And there is a tremendous spiritual exhilaration arising from this victory of the self over circumstance.

All these things, then, can be related to our own daily lives and the situations in which we find ourselves. I think that we participate in mystical experiences more than we realize. As a large and complete pattern, the mystical experience is probably a stranger to most, but as a series of continuing interior impulses, I suspect that it is not entirely strange to the average person. We all have moments in which it appears that our knowledge or our understanding transcends itself. There are times when our judgment is greater than we realize, when our decisions are better than we know. There are tremendous emergencies that we meet with a new courage, or a profound sense of value, which would not have been available to us a few hours before.

It would appear that we are subject to an insight due to a kind of disorientation that arises when we suddenly find ourselves inadequate. When we are suddenly aware that we have lost control of a situation, or lost control of ourselves, or that we face an unknown that is deeper than we can fathom, there is this moment of uncertainty and confusion in which our self-assurance breaks down. In this moment of hesitation, or disorientation, there seems to be a temporary weakening of the objective faculties; they lose their authority to dominate us. And it is in that moment, when the objective mind no longer has authority, that the subjective mind comes through, taking over this situation and bestowing the remedy, or giving us some insight as to what can solve our problem.

Visions of importance presented to us by the psychic nature are of very little value unless we are able to record them. Therefore, what we actually need is a kind of sleeping in which memory and certain other faculties are somewhat alert. If we have a total obliteration of faculties, we will have no adequate recollection of the dream. This is why the vision dream is most likely to occur, as we have mentioned, during the twilight hour. Other conditions may influence this, however. The individual may find that under pressure or worry, he does not sleep well, so that this condition of half sleeping and half waking may occur at other hours due to the disturbances of his life. But one apparent fact remains: namely, that the valid vision demands a certain degree of both subjective and objective awareness. It demands that the subjective be active and positive, and that the objective be partly active, but receptive. Thus we have the psychic experience coming from the invisible roots of the mind, to be recorded in the subtle substances of the brain itself. Unless this record is made, the project is imperfect.

The experience itself will very often be presented, as most dream phenomena, in a series of symbols. We should point out here that these symbols are not generated by the lower psyche. The genuine vision, or mystical dream, is quite different from the dream produced by the various afflictions and distortions of the psyche, by which its abnormalties are revealed. The type of dream to which we are now referring, sometimes called the archetypal dream, is directive. It is the kind of experience that is not to be regarded as an hallucination or merely a fantasy of sleep. It does not necessarily tell us what is the matter with us, although it may reveal by its message how to correct certain things that are wrong. This kind of dream comes to us out of the constructive, directive part of our own subjective nature. It is therefore a dream of authority, which expresses the will of our superior nature. And since this superior nature is more aware of truth or of reality than we normally are, it is customary to consider that such dreams are also indicative of the will of God, or the will of Truth.

The archetypal dream is usually accompanied by certain symptoms, or certain conditions, by which we are able to differentiate it from other dreams. For one thing, this dream is often described by the person who has it as a waking experience. He is loath to believe that he was asleep. He is inclined to feel that he awakened before the vision appeared. I have talked to many persons who have had this type of experience during sleeping hours—or when it would be normally assumed that they were asleep—and they insisted that they were awake when the experience happened. If they are then asked: "What did you do? Being awake, did you jump out of bed, did you sit up, did you reach for a pencil and paper to record this experience? What did you think, what did you feel?"— their answers to these questions are always dim and evasive. One individual will say, "Well, I didn't move; I couldn't move, because the experience itself seemed to paralyze me. I was conscious, but I could not move." Another will say, "When my eyes were open, I could see; I know I could see because I closed my eyes, and then the vision wasn't there; therefore, it had to be something that had a solidity outside of myself. But at the moment of the experience, I felt in a strange state of suspension. I knew I was awake, but I did not move; I did not want to move; I could not speak. All of the normal functions were suspended."

Occasionally, a dream of this kind, or a vision, will occur when some other person is in the room at the time. This is not common, but it does happen. I know of a case where an individual explained the vision and told of having apparently reacted quite physically, having been wide awake, and the witness stated definitely that the person was completely asleep through the entire process. Yet the person who had the vision could not believe that he was asleep.

Thus the vision differs from the ordinary dream in this peculiar validity of the sense of conscious awareness. It does not have the mysterious sense of merely being part of a shadow. It is not something through which the individual passes as an experience of a being moving through some strange region like the mysterious realms of Dante and Milton. The vision experience is something that happens to you; you know about it; it is meaningful.

Another characteristic of a vision is that it may be preceded by some rather mysterious situation. It is frequently preceded by a sense of extreme coldness or chill. Those who have recorded visions other than at night, who apparently have been picked up into a vision state while sitting at a table, or while reading a book, or something of this nature, nearly always report the sense of chill—a change in the atmosphere around them. What they are really telling us, of course, is that there is a change in the circulation of their own bodies. The circulation seems to retire from the periphery and center around certain vital areas of consciousness. This is also common to man in danger of shock. A person subjected to a sudden danger will often have the sense of chill. Certain types of illness also produce this feeling, which is generally regarded as a poor symptom. Actually, this sense of chill indicates a link with the condition of sleep. During sleep, there is a tendency for the body temperature to lower, but we are not usually aware of it.

Most of those who have had visions in a waking state also report that they experienced a certain sense of haziness, the approach of something resembling sleep. They were nodding, they were not fully objectively aware, and they were not usually engaged in any active enterprise at that moment. They were resting, contemplating, or absorbed in some thought or study.

Scientific research has established the fact that the material environment in which we live is carried into the brain in the form of impulses. We do not carry a picture of a chair or a table into the brain, although we seem to see it there. The eye picks up an image, transforms it into vibratory waves, and transfers these waves to the brain, where they are reassembled in the form of the object. This means that there is a form-creating process in the brain, so that vibrations striking the brain can be transformed into images by the innate processes of the brain. In view of this, there is no reason to doubt that an image projected from the interior part of man's psychic life and impressed upon the brain, can take form there and appear to be just as real as any physical thing the individual can see.

A proof of this process is hypnosis, where an imaginary person, suggested into existence by the hypnotist, may be placed among a group of real persons, and will be seen by the subject as part of the group of real persons. The imaginary person will fit completley into the scenery and landscape, and will be just as natural in appearance as the others. The person under the hypnotic influence will see the imaginary person mingling with the real persons, walking among them, appearing to pass behind one or in front of another, and his mental equipment will rationalize the entire situation so completely that he will be unable to determine which of the people in front of him are physical realities and which one is the imagined being.

In the same way, the hypnotist can block out one person from a group, so that of twelve persons, eleven will be visible, and the twelfth invisible. This invisible person will be in the room with all the others, conversing with them, walking among them, and be totally invisible to the hypnotized individual. The entire situation is controlled from the brain itself, and not by the sensory perceptions as we know them.

I believe it is reasonable to say, therefore, that in a dream or vision, forms are engendered in the brain as the result of vibratory mental image-patterns. We may then ask what these image-patterns might be that would cause this kind of a formation within the consciousness of a person. There are as yet no absolutely conclusive, formularized answers, but the process seems to be this: All thought, whether it arises from observation or from internal processes, is vibration. Thoughts have within themselves their own vibratory patterns and images. A thought, pressed upon the mind and transferred from the mind to the brain, must there clothe itself in the available materials from which the brain can derive its images. The brain cannot derive its images from any material that is not within its range of perception and reflection. In other words, if the brain of man is going to interpret any symbol or energy, or to give form to any abstract idea, it must clothe that abstraction in something which the brain itself has objectively experienced. It is perfectly possible, therefore, for the brain to bestow any form with which it is familiar, but it cannot bestow a form with which it is not familiar.

Now apparently, the most abstract form that the brain is capable of bestowing is simply light. The most abstract negation is darkness. Therefore, things otherwise beyond formation, beyond any experience by which form can be implied, have the tendency to appear as light, or as simple geometrical patterns arising in light or composed of light. These geometrical patterns are derived from basic psychic archetypes, but they must also exist in this world in order for the brain to be able to register them.

At a very primitive time in man's experience, his own mental processes apparently attempted to create a differentiating procedure by means of which things natural could in some way be mentally separated from things supernatural. The brain, unable to experience a supernatural thing, or to give form to a thing formless as far as faculties and perceptions are concerned, hit upon a strategy that has since been distributed throughout society—namely, to create extraordinary forms by making compounds of ordinary ones. A man walking along the street is a natural form; a horse galloping down the road is a natural form; but if we take the upper part of a man and put it onto the lower part of a horse, we have an unnatural form—in this case, a centaur—a form by which we can convey something that is not of this world. A centaur does not exist to our experience, yet it is composed of two creatures that do exist.

Thus we have the symbol of something unworldly, metaphysical, transcendental, by the simple contrivance of putting two natural forms into what the mind recognizes as an impossible combination. This is a very common symbolic process, and may have resulted in many of the ancient symbols that have descended to us from antiquity. Among the Chinese, the dragon was such a form. Among various peoples, satyrs and nymphs and mermaids were these unnatural forms. This is still used in the medicine rituals of primitive peoples, in the mask cult, where the individual becomes superhuman by wearing a mask that completely conceals his natural features and conveys the impression of a monstrous unnatural being. So in the subconscious vision-dream sequences, as for instance in the Apocalypse, we have a number of mysterious composite

creatures as symbols of ideas. We are reminded of the mysterious interpretation of the great figure in Nebuchadrezzar's dream. The King
dreamed of an extraordinary figure with head of gold and feet of clay,
and the image collapsed when the stone was cast against its feet. All the
soothsayers and interpreters of dreams and visions were invited to come
and explain this strange dream. And finally the prophet did so, and
gained great distinction in the land.

This kind of dream or experience appears to be archetypal, inasmuch
as it represents a meaning pressing from within, clothing itself in forms
different from those in nature, yet near enough to nature for man to
grasp their significance. It is another peculiarity of this type of vision
that the meaning is frequently communicated with the form. Part of the
process of interpretation is carried on subconsciously even before the
person having the vision is aware of the process. Other elements of the
interpretation become apparent to us from objective contemplation.
Applying the symbolism to known incidents in our own living gradually
reveals the meaning.

The archetypal dream, then, making use of innumerable subconscious
contrivances, takes from within the consciousness of the individual, and
is projected from there in one way or another. Sometimes the projection
is rather abstract and in itself mysterious. In many visions, the individual
feels himself projected into the vision. He feels, as Ezekiel did, that he is
suddenly in the midst of the world of his own dream. Yet this is no
common dream; this is not a dream involving just ordinary personal
problems. It is a cosmic dream—a dream of a universe made up of
wheels within wheels; a dream of the Merkabah of the Chariot of
Righteousness, borne upon the powers and wings of the cherubim, in
which sits the Master of the Mysteries. All these visions indicate
archetypal insight. They represent some psychic truth, some message,
trying to break through into objectivity. They are the means of
communicating the abstract to faculties that are unable to receive the
pressure of the abstract directly. The brain, in order to take hold of the
message, must be able to associate it with a pattern or symbol.

Ancient peoples, at a very early time, developed symbols, usually a
picture of the object they wished to represent. This was relatively simple.
It was somewhat more difficult, however, to symbolize actions,
especially if they involved a complicated procedure of some kind. And it
was really a challenge to the ingenuity of man to represent qualities, such
as virtue or honesty. Gradually, man had to develop abstract forms to
represent abstract concepts. These forms could not simply be shown to
someone without first giving him the key to their meanings. Thus, a
whole group of symbols appeared that had to be learned, or
remembered.

All invisible beings, principles, energies, and powers, came to be included among the abstract, or unobvious, forms; and the greatest surviving unobvious form of all is the form of God. Among most primitive peoples, there was no symbol for the Supreme Deity, because man could not even conceive an appropriate symbol. Finally the idea of no symbol suggested a crystallization or concretion of "no symbol" by simply taking an area and circumscribing it with a circle. The circle, therefore, became the symbol of infinity because it was an area in which there was nothing. This was the principle behind the use of certain jade implements in China, where the flat disc with the opening in the center became the symbol of Deity—the opening, or hollow, or empty place being the only possible symbol of God.

This process of primitive man learning how to transmit ideas is perhaps the same mystery of vocabulary that is involved in the human being's inner consciousness trying to press moral abstractions upon the objective mind. This process is in one direction—from the outer world into the core of man. A similar motion, but from another direction, is from a superior state above and beyond man downward into the core of man. It is as though man's psychic nature were like the middle point in an hour glass. Energies moving from above enter the brain, and have their impressions; energies moving from below enter the brain and have their impressions. In the vision, therefore, the energy from the superior part of consciousness moves in and imposes itself upon the brain processes, resulting in a number of possible manifestations.

We may also have an auditory type of experience, in which we see nothing, but hear something. This simply means that the brain has integrated vibration into sound, and we are hearing something from within ourselves, although it may appear to be coming to us from the outside. In this matter, of course, our common attitudes play a part. To our general thinking, sound must come from the outside, for noise is of the outside. It is therefore inconsistent with our common experience to assume that sound should come from an invisible silence within us. Moreoever, as the inner sound mingles with outer sounds, we are unable to distinguish the source of one from the source of the other. Thus we frequently assume that we hear things said around us that are really coming from within us.

The projection of images may be attributed to the same process. An individual looking at a wall, under certain conditions, may see an image appear upon that wall. This image may be animate, perform various actions, and even speak, but it is a projection from himself. The wall, however, is on the outside. Now, the combining of the wall and the interior image is like uniting two negatives in the production of a photograph in which two pictures are blended into one. In the case of the image on the wall, the union takes place within the ordering faculties of the brain. Naturally, the brain itself, being an instrument without self-knowledge, is not aware of its own inability to discriminate between the interior and the exterior picture. Therefore, the consciousness of man is inclined to interpret the entire situation as being external, because this is familiar and expected.

This takes us to another point that is frequently brought up in regard to visions. The individual having the vision is convinced that it must be on the outside, because when he opens his eyes, the vision is there, and when he closes his eyes, the vision is not there. This, however, is not borne out by mental experimentation. We must remember that the moment we test an inner experience by means of some function of our own, we are undoubtedly and inevitably determined to achieve certain results that will conform with our expectancies. The average person expects things seen to disappear when he closes his eyes; and because this expectancy exists in the subtle substance of mental material, it is immediately fulfilled. Also, the voluntary action of opening and closing the eyes, may be enough in itself to temporarily disturb the image.

The real answer to this is that the individual, being the internal controller of the whole process, is able to create any verisimilitude he wishes. If he insists that the image shall remain when his eyes are closed, it will remain. If he knows that it cannot remain, it will not remain. The mind is a magician in these things, and will accomplish whatever we demand of it. We know that under hypnosis, this acceptance of determination is instantaneous; therefore, it is useless to assume that we would have to argue ourselves into one concept or the other. That which we naturally accept will immediately and inevitably occur.

Actually, we have almost complete evidence that a vision is communicated to man only because man is man. We have never yet had true historical evidence of the intercession of Deity in the affairs of men, except through men. We do not have the experience of a man praying for financial help and having a hand reach down from heaven with a pocketbook in it. If the farmer prays for rain, it may rain; but the rain will be coming from clouds, not from a blue sky. And these clouds will gather according to their own laws and then precipitate. Man himself expects this help to occur or arise mysteriously, but he knows that this mystery will be associated with beings of his own kind; that where he needs help, help will come to him in a natural way. It is only the faith that it will occur in some supernatural way, that adds mystery to the simple circumstance.

The vision comes to the sensitive person, and is communicated from him to others who lack the sensitivity to have the experience themselves. Also, in some instances, the experience appears to occur to more than one person. This has long been a very difficult situation to explain, but psychology is beginning to pick up the threads. We now realize that what is termed the archetypal form, or the archetypal dream, arises from a pattern that exists in space. Under certain common problems, stress, or tension, this pattern may impinge itself upon more than one person at a time. There are instances, apparently, where it has impinged itself upon a multitude of persons at one time—each one seeing the same thing, but seeing from within himself. The agreement was in the archetype, and the archetype, imposed upon the consciousness of the individual, was sufficiently firm to produce a generally common experience. Each person saw within himself that which others saw within themselves; but since each also beheld the appearance as though outside of himself, we have the phenomenon of the multitude seeing at once.

I knew of one very good report of such a case, where several hundred persons saw the same thing at the same time. But these several hundred persons were among probably a hundred thousand persons—the rest not seeing it at all. If the event had been a completley physical, optical experience, all persons—except perhaps a very small group defective in their optical equipment—would have seen it. Again, in a case where seven men standing on a ship all see a phantom ship, but seven more men standing alongside them see nothing, we must assume that an archetype of some kind has impressed those seven men. It is the only way we can seriously seek to solve the problem, for if the ship had actually been there, it would have been equally visible to all persons with equal optical equipment; they would all have seen it.

There is indication, as in what are called the "apocalyptical visions," that an archetype in nature gradually develops or unfolds to a degree of near completeness, so that this archetype has a highly involved symbolism of its own. The archetypal symbols are set within the function of a universal mind, operating similarly to man's mind, but also in the process of transforming abstractions into orderly symbolic patterns. Under certain conditions, these collective archetypes can be impressed upon a number of minds simultaneously, and minds of a certain degree of sensitivity will receive them, whereas other minds will not.

We know this is true in practically every field of human activity. What we term the law of exception depends upon the fact that even the most common circumstances cannot always be depended upon to occur to all persons. A certain remedy against an ailment may cure ninety cases and leave ten untouched. Or a new drug may help fifty people, injure twenty, and have no effect upon thirty. The reasons for these differences lie within the person, and not within the drug. The drug is an inanimate, impersonal thing, but it has to operate upon animate, personalized creatures; and their reactions depend upon themselves. A powerful impulse—an archetype or folk image—arising in Universal Mind, is itself impressed upon various persons. Some record it, some do not; some distort it. To some, it is a great and wonderful experience; to others, a terrible and dangerous experience. All depends upon the integration of the being upon whose abstract mental structure the impression is made.

Generally speaking, then, I think we can say that the vision is nature's method of conveying some form of knowledge, some way of knowing, beyond the normal capacity of the individual to comprehend. To do this, several factors are introduced. One is shock or stress, by which the entire experience is made important as being unusual, unique, or totally different. The second important factor is that it occurs to the person himself. It is not reported; it is not communicated. It is something about which the person afterwards feels that he knows it because it has happened to him.

The third point is that the vision must interpret itself in materials available for such interpretation. Where the materials are available, they will be used. Where they are not available, materials relatively available will be grouped together in a new pattern, in order that they may be the vehicle for an extraordinary idea. This very grouping, visualized by the individual within himself, becomes extremely important because it is strange or different. It challenges his imagination and his thought, and invites him to the definite consideration of the experience as being valid or important in itself.

We know, for example, that in many parts of the world where Christianity has sent its missionaries, persons coming under the influence of the Christian faith have mystical experiences. They have them in other religions also, but the point of interest is that nearly always, where a person of one of these other groups has a vision relating to Christianity, this vision is invested with the forms natural to that person. Mystics of China, for instance, who have had visions of Jesus and have drawn pictures of their visions, always represented Jesus as Chinese. He had to be, because he was drawn out of their own subconscious repository; they had to clothe him in the forms that they knew and understood.

Not all visions, of course, are valid. But where the vision is genuine, it nearly always carries a sense of authenticity. It is meaningful, reasonable, and proper. It is solutional. It has a mark of validity, as though it were sealed by the very seal of God. The individual is not even inclined to resist or doubt it. Its peculiar clarity and integrity come through to him. The true vision occurs when man is receptive and quiet, has entered the stillness, and is seeking to know the truth; or in those hours when this stillness is imposed upon him by nature, so that he is open to the imposition of a spiritual factor.

One of the great keys that has been closed down through the ages in determining the validity of visions, is the consequence. A vision must be considered valid if it changes the life of the person for the better. The vision of St. Francis of Assisi, for example, took him out of a life of dissipation and intemperance and sanctified him to the best that he knew in the way of service to the need of his fellow men. If a vision brings great understanding, philosophic insight, or advances man's knowledge of things factual, it must be recognized as genuine. Those types of inner experiences of an auditory nature that were given to the great composers, by which they were able to bring through into objectivity melodies and marvelous harmonies, were certainly great mystical happenings. All of these things relate to the availability within man of a superior power capable of being released at need, or under certain circumstances, for the preservation or the improvement of his life, or the service of his world. Where visions have led to great improvement, there is very little to be gained by doubting them.

If, however, visions or mystical experiences do not lead to improvement, if they merely lead to fanaticism or mania, there is still no need to use such instances as a disproof of visions. This merely proves that these experiences can arise either from the lower or from the higher psychic nature. When they arise from the lower nature, regardless of the picturesqueness they present, they tell the story of our sickness or our trouble. When they arise from the higher nature of man, they tell the story of his hopes, his aspirations, his inner resources. They indicate the spiritual destiny which is his in life. They are the call to the recognition of higher levels of being, of purpose, of achievement, or realization, than the individual has formerly known. Under these conditions, whether during sleeping or waking hours, the vision becomes a vital experience.

INDEX

Abstract symbolism 77-80
Accident, dream of 66
Accidents, symbolism of 63
Adventure, as symbol 50
Aesculapius 58
Aesop's fables 41
Afterlife, Egyptian concept of 11
Akashic record 67
American Indians: and dreams 69;
   hypnotic trances of, 9, 27
Amfortis dream 36
Animal symbolism 44-47
Animals and:
   dreams, 2-3; neurosis, 17; nocturnal
   activity, 19; sleep, 17
Animals, domestic, as symbols 47-48
Apocalypse of St. John 73
Apocalyptical visions 81
Archetypal:
   concepts, 41; consciousness, 30
   dreams, 74-75, 78; energy, 64;
   images and karma, 67; images and
   vision, 31
Archetypes:
   and inner life, 29; in visions, 81;
   symbolism of, 81
Aristotle 1
Assassins, sect of 8
Association and symbolism 40, 47
Auditory experiences 79
Awakening: psychology of, 23;
   significance of, 34

Battles, as symbol 50
Birds in symbolism 44-45
Birth and twilight hour 22
Blood and telepathy 68
Brain, impressions on 79
Brain and:
   auditory experience, 79; psychic
   sympathy, 68; sleep, 16; symbolism,
   77; vibrations, 76; visions, 74

Centaur, symbolism of 77
Childishness 49
Child-likeness 49
Children, as symbols 49
Chill, sense of, in visions 75
Chimera 43
Church, symbolism of 52,61
Cicero 26
Circle, symbolism of 79

Clairvoyance: and sleep, 10;
   in dreams, 68
Clothing, as symbol 48
Composite symbols 43, 77
Conscience: in symbolism, 48;
   process of, 28-29
Consciousness: during sleep, 24-25;
   in visions, 74
Culture and symbolism 41-42

Dated dreams 62
Daydreaming 5
Daylight and sleep 18
Death: and twilight hour, 22;
   compared with sleep, 9-11
Defense mechanisms 58
Delphi: Oracle of, 8; priestesses of, 26
Democritus 1
Destiny and karma 67
Disaster dreams 40-41, 53-56, 60-63
Dragon, as symbol 45, 77
Dream, meaning of word 1
Dream symbols, derivation of 33, 41
Dreams:
   as escape mechanism, 5; as psychotherapy, 61; causes of, 52; classification of, 3-4, 42-43; cosmic, 78;
   dated, 62; faces in, 43-44; influence
   on waking state, 40; mystical, 4,
   70-73; prodromic, 58; repetition of,
   34; resistance to, 56
Dreams and:
   age, 2; animals, 2-3; archetypal
   insight, 78; clairvoyance, 68-69;
   ESP, 68; foreknowledge, 27-28;
   knowledge, 4, 13-14; neurosis,
   13-14; physical handicaps, 3; psychic
   stress, 5-6; psychotherapy, 28, 60-61;
   sleep intensity, 21; telepathy, 68-69;
   twilight hours, 23-24; warnings,
   27-28
Dreams of:
   disaster, 40-41, 53-56, 60-63
   frustration, 50-51; Last Judgment,
   54; self-destruction, 49-50; wounds,
   36-37
Drowning, as symbol 51
Drugs and visions 8
Druids 8
Duel, as symbol 50
Dying in dreams 49-50

84

Eagle, as symbol 45
Earth energy 18-19; and twilight, 22
Earthquake of Martinique 62-63
Egyptian view of:
    afterlife, 11; sleep, 11, 22;
    twilight, 23-24
Elders, as symbols 48
Elementary forces, as symbols 46
Elephant, as symbol 46
Energy: earth, lunar, solar 18-19
Environment: and dreams, 2; and
    symbolism, 41
Equilibrium, point of 22-23
Escape mechanism 5
Expectancy factor in visions 81
Extrasensory faculties 62
Extrasensory perception and
    dreams 67-69
Ezekiel, vision of 78

Faces in dreams 43-44
Fasting and sleep 9
Fear mechanism, effects of 54-55
Flowers in symbolism 44
Foreknowledge:
    and karma, 67; and the subcon-
    scious, 66; in dreams, 27-28, 61, 63
Fortune telling 64
Frustration in symbolism 50-51

Geometrical patterns, as symbols 77
God: symbol for, 79; visions as will
    of, 74
Greek:
    oracles, 8, 26; view of dreams, 1;
    view of sleep, 11, 13
Grimm's fairy tales 43

Habit patterns 65
Hashish, use of 8
Health, dreams about 58-59
    (see also prodromic dreams)
Heartbeat, in sleep 16
Helpful symbols 42
Home, in symbolism 47
House, wrong, symbolism of 61
Hypnosis: and society, 30; mental
    rationalization in, 76
Hypnotic trances, 8; of American
    Indians, 27; of Greek oracles, 8

Inferiority complex 35
Infinity, symbol for 79
Insanity, veneration of 27

Intuition: as judgment 65-66; as
    protector, 32

Jack and Beanstalk symbolism 35-36
Judgment and intuition 65-66

Karma: and destiny, 67-68; and fore-
    knowledge, 67
Knowledge and:
    dreams, 13-14; sleep, 11; the sub-
    conscious, 28-29, 58-59, 60-61;
    visions, 82

Last Judgment, dreams of 54
Life, as symbol 51
Light, as symbol 77
Lunar energy, nature of 19

Malevolent symbols 3
Marriage, multiple 34
Meditation and sleep 11, 21
Memory 12; and symbols, 39;
    warnings of, 29
Metabolism and sleep 16, 19-21
Miracles 66
Mischievous symbols 42
Multiple vision phenomena 81-82
Music and visions 83
Mysterious symbols 42
Mystical experience 4, 82; in daily life,
    73; of Plotinus, 72-73; of St. Paul,
    70-72
Mythical creatures in symbolism 45-46
Mythology and dream symbols 33

Nuerosis and:
    animals, 16-17; dreams, 13-14;
    environment, 17-18; sleep, 18
Night worker: and sleep 20; and
    twilight hour, 24-25
Nirvanic trance 11

Objective faculties and:
    dreams, 21-22; sleep, 9; vision, 74
Oracles, Greek: accuracy of, 26;
    trances of, 8
Overself in dreams 60
Owl, as symbol 45

Paracelsus, concept of sympathy 68
Personality problems, and basic causes
    34-35
Planetary influence: as precipitating
    cause, 63-64; on sleep patterns, 20

Manly P. Hall, whose public career began in 1920, has delivered over eight thousand lectures in the United States and abroad and is the author of over 150 books and essays. His most popular work has been in continuous print since 1928—*The Secret Teachings of All Ages, An Encyclopedic Outline of Masonic, Hermetic, Qabbalistic, & Rosicrucian Symbolical Philosophy.*

In 1934 Manly P. Hall founded the Philosophical Research Society in Los Angeles, California, dedicating it to an idealistic approach to the solution of human problems. Nonsectarian and entirely free from educational, political, or ecclesiastical control, the Society's programs stress the need for the integration of philosopy, religion, and the science of psychology into one system of instruction. A unique feature is the PRS Library, an outstanding public facility devoted to source materials in obscure fields, with many rare and scarce items now impossible to obtain in the original.

Books by Manly P. Hall

Adventures in Understanding
Alchemy, A Comprehensive Bibliography of the
*   Manly P. Hall Collection of Books & Manuscripts*
America's Assignment with Destiny
Arhats of Buddhism
Astrological Keywords
Buddhism & Psychotherapy
Death to Rebirth
Dream Symbolism
First Principles of Philosophy
Freemasonry of the Ancient Egyptians
The Guru, By His Disciple
Healing, The Divine Art
Initiates of Greece & Rome
Invisible Records of Thought & Action
Lectures on Ancient Philosophy
Light of the Vedas
Lost Keys of Freemasonry
Man, Grand Symbol of the Mysteries
Masonic Orders of Fraternity
Meditation Symbols in Eastern & Western Mysticism
Mystical Christ
Mystics & Mysteries of Alexandria
Mystics of Islam
Old Testament Wisdom
Orders of the Great Work—Alchemy
Orders of the Quest—The Holy Grail
Orders of the Universal Reformation—Utopias
Paracelsus, His Mystical & Medical Philosophy
Pathways of Philosophy
The Phoenix, An Illustrated Review of Occultism
*   & Philosophy*
Questions & Answers
Reincarnation, The Cycle of Necessity
Rosicrucians & Magister Christoph Schlegel
Sages & Seers
Sages of China
Secret Destiny of America
The Secret Teachings of All Ages: An Encyclopedic
*   Outline of Masonic, Hermetic, Qabbalistic,*
*   & Rosicrucian Philosophy*
Self-Unfoldment by Disciplines of Realization
Shadow Forms
Story of Astrology
Studies in Character Analysis
The Tarot, An Essay
Twelve World Teachers
Venerated Teachers of the Jains, Sikhs, and Parsis
"Very Unusual"—The Wonderful World of Mr. K. Nakamura
Way of Heaven
Ways of the Lonely Ones
Words to the Wise

Write or telephone for complete catalog:
THE PHILOSOPHICAL RESEARCH SOCIETY, INC.
3910 Los Feliz Boulevard
Los Angeles, CA 90027-2399
From Outside California: (800) 548-4062
Californians: (213) 663-2167